THE LIFE AND TIMES OF
TYCHO BRAHE

Tyge Brahe, Astronomer, (1546-1601)

The Life
and Times of
Tycho Brahe

By JOHN ALLYNE GADE

PRINCETON UNIVERSITY PRESS

PRINCETON

FOR THE

AMERICAN–SCANDINAVIAN FOUNDATION

NEW YORK

1947

Printed in the United States of America
by Princeton University Press at Princeton, New Jersey

TO

Custode Harald Mortensen

OF THE ROYAL LIBRARY OF COPENHAGEN,

SCHOLARLY AND GENEROUS STUDENT

OF TYCHO BRAHE

PREFACE

HE year 1946 marked the four-hundredth anniversary of the birth of one of Scandinavia's greatest scientists, Tycho Brahe. These pages are thus intended as a quadricentennial tribute to the man, together with a description of the times in which he lived. Knowing little of astronomy, I have hazarded only what must be considered a superficial account of his scientific work, though not, I trust, an inaccurate one, for the manuscript has been checked by competent astronomers.

In the sixteenth century there was fortunately a universal brotherhood of scholarship in Europe, so that Tycho's astonishing researches and discoveries caused a great stir throughout the learned world of his day. For these reasons European libraries are fairly rich in literature pertaining to them. There is, however, less that is readable and readily available concerning the details of his very interesting personal life and character, especially in English. This book humbly assumes to supply some of these details for the general reader.

I am deeply indebted to the Royal Library of Copenhagen for many courtesies. No one could have been kinder than *Overbibliotekar* Paulli, and no one more helpful than *Custode* Harald Mortensen, to whom Tycho Brahe has been a religion ever since his early boyhood. Dr. Roy K. Marshall of the Franklin Institute of Philadelphia has likewise been so good as to correct "astronomical" errors in my manuscript, and Professor Leslie A. Marchand of Rutgers University has given it a general editing and revision to improve the literary style. I am also deeply indebted to Professor Robert Herndon Fife of Columbia University for his kindly assistance in the revision of the manuscript, as well as to Miss Gerda M. Andersen for her many corrections of it. Acknowledgment is further due to Miss Cicely Veronica Wedgwood and her publishers, the Yale University

Press, for permission to quote from her book *The Thirty Years'
War*, and to Mr. Alfred Noyes and his publishers, J. B. Lippincott & Co., who have been good enough to extend the same
privilege in regard to lines from *The Torch Bearers*.

J. A. G.

Château de Leefdael, Brabant
August 1946

CONTENTS

PAGE

Preface   vii

CHAPTER I

The sixteenth century. Tycho Brahe's historical and cultural
background   3

CHAPTER II

The Brahe family. Tycho's early studies at Copenhagen.
Sidelights on contemporary university life. In Leipzig with
Anders Sørensen Vedel. Death of his Uncle Jørgen   11

CHAPTER III

Tycho in Wittenberg and Rostock. Duel with Parsbjerg.
Life in Augsburg. Return to Scania in 1571. Death of his
father, Otto Brahe. Discovery of the new star, November
11, 1572. Tycho marries Kirstine   33

CHAPTER IV

Lectures at Copenhagen September 1574 to spring 1575.
Travels in Germany and Italy. Tycho accepts King Frederik II's offer of Hveen and settles there in 1576. Construction of Uraniborg and Stjerneborg   53

CHAPTER V

Cordial relations with Frederik II. Customs of the day.
Birth of Christian IV; Tycho casts his horoscope. His views
on astrology. Tycho on the crest of the wave. Sources of
income. Life and work at Hveen. Family, pupils, retainers   75

CHAPTER VI

Tycho's printing press and paper mill. Publications. Correspondence and visitors. Death of Frederik II in 1588   99

CHAPTER VII

Christian IV and James VI of Scotland visit Hveen. James'
marriage to Princess Anne of Denmark. Tycho as apothecary and medicus. He neglects the duties inherent in his
privileges. New works printed at Uraniborg   117

CONTENTS

PAGE

CHAPTER VIII

Tycho loses royal favor; is deprived of some of his fiefs; leaves Hveen April 29, 1597. Wrangle with Gellius Sascerides over daughter Magdalene's dowry. Tycho attempts work at Copenhagen   137

CHAPTER IX

Copenhagen in the sixteenth century. Tycho at Rostock with his family. Attempt at conciliating Christian IV. Stay at Wandsbeck. Governor Henrik Rantzau. Publication of *Astronomiæ instauratæ mechanica*, 1598. Visit to Wittenberg and stay with Professor Jessen   149

CHAPTER X

In Prague with Rudolph II, 1599. Life at Castle Benatky. Johann Kepler. Tycho's daughter, Elisabet, marries Franz Tengnagel. Work on Rudolphine Tables   169

CHAPTER XI

Tycho dies October 24, 1601. Kepler's description of his last days. Evaluation of Tycho's work and significance as an astronomer   185

Appendix. Brief account of Tycho Brahe's offspring   193

Bibliography   195

Index   205

ILLUSTRATIONS

FACING
PAGE

Tyge (Tycho) Brahe. Drawing in silverpoint by Tobias Gemperlin. Danish State Collection of Engravings at Copenhagen [*frontispiece*]

Tycho's great quadrant executed in Augsburg. From a model one-twentieth the size of the original, in the Historical Astronomical Collections at the Round Tower in Copenhagen   36

Tycho Brahe's celestial globe. From an engraving (The globe was burned in the big Copenhagen fire of 1728)   37

Plan of Uraniborg with cross section of cellars. Woodcut in *Mechanica* 1598   52

Map of Hveen at Tycho's time. From an engraving   52

Uraniborg and grounds. The castle was surrounded by flower gardens and orchards. The east gate is seen close to the bottom in the illustration. To the right, the servants' quarters; to the left, the printing establishment. After Tycho Brahe's *Mechanica*   53

Mural quadrant at Uraniborg. From an engraving in *Mechanica*   68

Bird's eye view of Stjerneborg with plan   69

Instrument (armilla) from Stjerneborg. Woodcut in *Epistolæ astronomicæ*, Uraniburgum 1588   100

Portrait of King Christian IV of Denmark. Painting by Karel van Mander, about 1640. From a painting at Frederiksborg burned 1859   101

Portrait of Tycho Brahe. Painted by Gemperlin. Frame designed by G. Heilmann   116

Portrait of Tycho Brahe. With the Brahe arms in left corner. From a painting by Gemperlin. Burned at Frederiksborg 1859   116

[xi]

Tycho Brahe's autograph. Uraniborg 1589. "Medullas non Cortices" (Not the shells but the kernels)   117

Facsimile of the title page of *Astronomiae instauratae mechanica*. Wandesburgi 1598. Dedicated to Emperor Rudolph II   148

Facsimile of Johann Kepler's entry in the *Register of Observations* about Tycho's last illness and death.   149

Tycho Brahe's tombstone with his effigy. In the Teyn Church at Prague. The inscription reads: "In A.D. 1601 on October 24, the noble, well-born Lord, Tycho Brahe, Master of Knudstrup, *Praeces* Uraniborg, *Conciliarius* to His Holy Imperial Majesty, died, and here his bones rest"   164

The Teyn Church in Prague   164

Excavation of Stjerneborg 1901   165

Ruins of Uraniborg 1846. Southeast earthen wall. From a drawing   165

CHAPTER ONE

The heavens declare the glory of God; and the firmament sheweth his handywork. . . .

In them hath he set a tabernacle for the sun, which is as a bridegroom coming out of his chamber, and rejoiceth as a strong man to run a race.

His going forth is from the end of the heaven, and his circuit unto the ends of it: and there is nothing hid from the heat thereof.—PSALM 19:1, 4-6

HE sixteenth century was one of the most inter-
esting in the history of Europe. At its turn the
previous conception of the world was shattered.
During its latter half the renaissance of Scandinavia took place. Tycho Brahe lived in this
intellectually fertile half-century. In it Denmark became one of
the great European sea powers, twice its present size. The Hanseatic League was broken, and the pirates who had so long
haunted the Baltic were exterminated, so that, as a token of the
Danish king's right to rule the northern seas, all foreign ships
passing through the Sound were forced to strike their topsails to
Danish men-of-war.

In addition to the crown of Denmark proper, her king also
wore that of Norway and owned the lovely, fertile provinces of
Halland, Blekinge and Scania, now belonging to Sweden. Denmark could thus close the Sound to all enemies at will, while
Sweden, on the other hand, lacked natural geographical frontiers. The duchies of Slesvig and Holstein, with the mighty free
city of Hamburg as their southern neighbor, likewise belonged
to the Danish Crown.

It was a singularly lovely country that surrounded the water-
ways leading to the Baltic, covered with forests teeming with
boars and stags and wolves. Of its million people, the capital,
Copenhagen, had some thirteen thousand inhabitants and was
thus second after Bergen among northern cities. Much of the
population of the Danish capital was composed of Dutch and
German immigrants, huddled together for protection rather
than for social intercourse.

Denmark's rise and decline were due to various factors. During Tycho's lifetime two kings sat on her throne, Frederik II
and Christian IV,[1] both great monarchs in their different ways.

---

[1] Frederik II, 1559-1588; Christian IV, 1588-1648.

They, as well as their predecessors of the House of Oldenburg, were more or less German. Both Frederik and his son married German princesses and spoke and wrote the language as much as their own tongue. Frederik was even born in Germany. No other Danish king was ever so beloved by his people as he, not because he was one of the few, if not the only, king of the Oldenburg line who had no illicit liaisons, but rather because of his genial and unaffected manner and the common sense and self-denial he exhibited in giving full scope to well-selected ministers whose efficiency in their various departments he frankly recognized and supported, irrespective of personal prejudices. His father, Christian III,[2] had been surrounded by great statesmen and admirals, such as Johan Friis, Peder Oxe, Herluf Trolle and Peder Skram, and Frederik was similarly fortunate in being able to lean upon the equally talented Niels Kaas, Jørgen Rosenkrantz, Christofer Valkendorf and Henrik Rantzau. Peder Oxe proved of great assistance to him too in bringing the finances of the realm into order. Though Frederik and his councilors were forced to abandon their dream of reestablishing the Kalmar Union and once again uniting Denmark, Norway and Sweden under one crown, and though the Seven Years' War ended disastrously for Denmark, Frederik at least succeeded in maintaining his nation's supremacy in the north.

When Frederik's son, the magnificent and joyous Christian IV, who was only twelve years old at his father's death in 1588, ascended the throne in 1596, his energetic hand was felt in everything. In foreign policy his influence was immediately sensed; he instituted a series of domestic reforms and attempted to improve trade and industry by abolishing the still-remaining privileges of the Hanseatic cities and encouraging the wholesale immigration of skillful and well-to-do Dutch traders and handicraftsmen into Denmark under most favorable conditions. The reorganization of the army and rebuilding of the navy were among his achievements.

[2] Christian III, 1534-1559.

In Denmark, as in Sweden, the progress of the Reformation had been far more rapid than in Germany. Luther's friend and disciple, Bugenhagen, had, at the king of Denmark's instance, drawn up a plan of religious doctrine, worship and discipline that was given formal sanction by an assembly of the Danish States at Odense as early as 1539. The revolt against certain doctrines and practices of the Roman Catholic Church and the universal supremacy of the Papacy swept rapidly through Denmark, and the sovereign took the lead in establishing separate ecclesiastical bodies on national lines, as opposed to centralized church government. The increased revenue derived from the appropriation of church property was of immense value and relief to the Crown, which through successive reigns had been chronically impoverished. Fortunately, such of the large funds as the grasping nobles did not get into their hands were well and wisely applied.

On the other hand, Denmark's subsequent decline may be largely attributed to her wars in Sweden and Germany, and her own form of government. During the sixteenth century the monarchy had slowly risen in Denmark on the ruins of feudalism. But while in Sweden hereditary monarchy had been established, and the king was no longer dependent upon the noble for his election, such was not the case in Denmark. There the privy council, the *Rigsraad*, was really the permanent owner of the realm and the Crown lands, and the king was merely the administrator. On his accession, each king was liable to be bound by a new charter (*Haandfæstning*). While there were no noble as mighty as or mightier than the king, like the Guises of Condés of France, the nobility were the true rulers in Denmark throughout many years of the sixteenth century, years which were thus known as *Adelsvældet*, or the period of nobility rule. The previous aristocracy was being transformed into an oligarchy.

The estates of the nobles, many of them similar to the Crown lands and many of them seized from the Catholic Church, con

posed about one-half the area of Denmark, and the owners, an exclusive and selfish aristocracy, well-advanced in decadence, were in many respects independent of the central government, both as regards taxation and administration. While many of these families died out, either in war, in killing each other, in the plagues, or by constant excesses, the fittest survived. It must, however, be said in their defense that, taken all in all, they were a better lot than noblemen elsewhere in Europe, both as to education and as to knowledge and manners, some of which they had acquired by foreign study and travel. There were some four thousand of them, always intermarrying, and, aside from the king, possessing most of the riches and privileges of the country. They occupied all the well-paid and important government offices, paid no taxes, received freely a portion of the labor of those who lived on their fiefs, had free access to plenty of excellent fishing and hunting and were the recipients of tithes on certain church property. In return, their only obligation was to arm their peasants in time of war and to fight at their head.

This was the scene in which Tycho Brahe was raised and these were the men from whom he sprang. Their claims and privileges naturally endangered the economic and political interest of the state and the nation. All people below the king and the nobles were classed together as "subjects." First in the humble scale came the clergy, who with the Reformation had ceased to exist as a spiritual estate though still represented in the *Rigsdag*, or Diet. Its members were the preachers and teachers, looked down upon by their betters. Below them were the burgesses, who had suffered frightfully during the Count's War (*Grevens Fejde*), and finally the lowest and most miserable of all, the peasants, who had sunk to the level of bondsmen without any political rights whatsoever.

If we look further afield than Tycho's own country, we find that the second half of the sixteenth century was not only a tremendous and restless epoch in European development but one of the most remarkable periods in the history of civilization.

[6]

The Holy Roman emperors gained their crowns through un-holy alliances, bribery and double-dealing. The restless Turk was a constant menace. A determined and profane little red-headed queen of England saw her brave sea-dogs and adventurers humble the mightiest empire of her time and sink and scatter around her tight little isle an armada great beyond the imaginings of sailors. Across the Channel, her nearest neighbor fought and murdered without respite and, after the night of St. Bartholomew, made the whole Christian world either shudder or applaud. Brantôme viewed with cynical indifference the crimes and vices of the last of the Valois. Calvin hurled his denunciations across the Alps; the northern United Provinces of the Lowlands retrieved their independence. The great Charles V's only son labored to destroy everything resembling free institutions, and the Inquisition, though abating its bloody fury, maintained yet its severe and watchful control over the least suspicion of heresy. Though the finest flowering of the Renaissance was past, the Medicis still sat on their glorious Florentine throne.

Despite their wars and rumors of wars, these decades also produced very great men. Genius was at its flood. Shakespeare, Drake and Tycho Brahe were contemporaries. Cervantes during these years told the tale of the Knight of La Mancha, Spenser that of the Faerie Queene, and Bacon sought elusive truths. Titian, Veronese, Rubens and Michelangelo painted and carved their masterpieces. Giordano Bruno died a martyr to free thought, while Galileo, Brahe and Kepler solved the enigmas of the starry heavens, and Copernicus' work became the cornerstone of modern astronomy.

CHAPTER TWO

Let now the astrologers, the star-gazers, the monthly prognosticators, stand up, and save thee from these things that shall come upon thee.—
ISAIAH 47:13

HE Brahe family was of old and distinguished nobility.[1] Its members had for generations served king and country in council and on the battlefield. There was a Swedish as well as a Danish branch of the family. One of the Swedish Brahes, Ebba, became the love of the great Gustavus Adolphus' life, while two Per Brahes, as well as a Magnus and a Niels, rose to prominent positions in Sweden. Per the Elder, who was one of Gustavus I's senators, lived during the greater portion of Tycho's life. Even today several Danish castles carry the Brahe name and one of the great families hyphenates the names of Tycho's parents, Bille and Brahe. In his own time, though intermarriage in the high aristocracy had been too frequent to keep its branches virile and strong, the women of the family must have been a stout lot, for they often bore a dozen children, most of whom seemed to survive the ignorance of hygiene and lack of nursery care of those "good old days" and grew into fine men and women.

Married women were then often referred to by their maiden name plus the genitive suffix of their husband's. Thus Beate Bille was referred to as "Beate Bille, Otto's," while the children, after the family name, added their father's. You were thus Tycho Brahe Ottosøn, or Margrete Brahe Otto's daughter.

Tycho, the first-born son, who came into the world on a December day in 1546, was named, as was the custom, for his grandfather. The latter was a great "swell" who had received from his betrothed a sheet bordered with twenty pearls, sewn on by her own fingers. Tycho's mother, Beate, reared Elisabet, Tyge,[2] Steen, Marin, Axel, Margrete, Kirstine, Jørgen

---

[1] In Denmark the nobles carried no titles until 1671. They were called "free and well-born" or "good men."

[2] Many of the noblemen of the day wrote their names in several ways, either because it took their fancy or because they were not quite sure how they last had written it. In writing Latin our astronomer signed "Tycho," in writing Danish "Tyge."

(George), Knud, and finally the youngest, Sofie, born in 1556. So there should be no doubt as to his being the oldest son, Tycho writes:

Est ego Brahæus de quinis fratribus unus
Et genitus primo, vix repudatus eram.

He had a still-born twin brother, for whose tombstone he, later in life, composed the following astonishing inscription in Latin verse:

"I who am dead have been resurrected. I was buried in this earth before I was born. Guess then who I was? I was unborn in my mother's womb, when death became my door to life. There was another enclosed with me, a brother who still lives, for I was a twin. God granted him a longer life than me, so that he might see the strange things on the earth and in the heavens. My fate has not been worse than his. He lives on earth, but I in heaven. He is subject on earth to a thousand perils, that happen on land, at sea, and in the stars. But I am with God in heaven where I enjoy everlasting peace and joy. When he [Tycho] finally rests his tired limbs under the cold earth, then we will both be united in heaven and he will participate in everlasting joy. Until then he will have to bear patiently the body's burden and not envy me my joy. Owing to my sudden death I was denied a name among the living. He instead of me bears the name of my grandfather. My grandfather's name was Tyge and his surname Brahe, and my brother also is named Tyge. It is he who has honored my grave with these verses. He is now twenty-five years old."

While such an effort might in our day indicate that its author was out of his senses, this was far from the case in the sixteenth century. The twins, both the dead and the living one, were thought of sympathetically by those who read the epitaph.

Tycho's father, Otto Brahe *til* Knudstrup, was a privy councilor, and after having served as lieutenant of various counties was appointed governor of the important castle of Helsingborg in Scania, controlling the Sound opposite Elsinore, while his mother, Beate, in 1592 succeeded his aunt and foster-mother, Inger Oxe, as Queen Sophia's Mistress of the Robes. His brother Steen became a privy councilor and commandant of Kalundborg, a port on the west coast of Sjælland. Another brother, Knud, likewise became a member of the king's council and one of his most intimate advisers. Jørgen, who married Inger Oxe, also took his place in public affairs. Contemporary history speaks of them as *de lystige Braher*, "the jolly Brahes," so they must have had a lot of fun in them and have been pleasant people to associate with. A stout and fine race! It was a strange trick of fate that one of them, whose name was to prove one of the very greatest in Danish history, was to choose a career despised and looked down upon by the entire tribe, with only one or two exceptions.

At such times as Otto's family did not accompany him to his post at Helsingborg, they lived in the little Knudstrup castle, built in a small lake and approached by a bridge. All around it were far-flung, rustling Scania wheatfields, birch and beech hemming them in. There Beate bore the twins, on December 14, 1546,[3] only a few months after the death of Martin Luther. "One of them," says the chronicle, "to be named Tycho, after his grandfather who fell at Malmö in 1523, survived, while the other, seemingly worthless, was buried." Nearby lived the uncle, Jørgen, or George, Brahe, who, being childless, was lonely and wanted little Tycho the moment he was shown him. The parents naturally would hear of no such nonsense, but what he could not obtain by fair means Jørgen intended to obtain by foul. At an unguarded moment, when Otto was at his post and Beate away from the castle, Jørgen abducted the babe, rode home with him and locked his castle gates.

Needless to say, a frightful family row ensued. But, follow-

[3] Otto's family records state: "In the year of our Lord 1546 my son Tyge was born between 9 and 10 in the morning."

ing the usual course of events, Beate soon conceived anew, and this time another boy was successfully brought into the world, casting rather a different light upon the matter. The brothers agreed to discuss the dilemma in a dispassionate manner. With the arrival of the new baby, Otto had at least one son at Knudstrup, with every chance of more to come; Jørgen had none and no hopes. He had, on the other hand, wealth and large estates, and the adoption, care and education of Tycho would probably mean the boy would be his heir. "One son, more or less, what does it matter to you?" Jørgen urged. Agreement was reached, and Tycho knew nothing of the dispute in which he had played so early and so essential a part. He was aware only of the love of his Uncle Jørgen and Aunt Inger throughout his childhood.

As the boy emerged from the nursery to the schoolroom and a tutor was engaged on his seventh birthday, Tycho showed that he had brains and plenty of them. In addition, therefore, to elementary lessons, riding and the use of the sword, he was taught Latin and other preparatory subjects requisite for a future statesman. As soon as he knew enough Latin[4] his tutor was pleased to help the little fellow in his attempts at making Latin verses. As in France and Germany, versifying on every possible occasion was much in vogue among the Danish gallants as well as the scholars. The boy must have heard his elders read poems they were constantly receiving, so he also wanted to have his try at the art. Unfortunately, his tutor could not have been a man of either force or character, for his charge was allowed far too often to have his own way, an indulgence that later in life was to cause Tycho much trouble and distress. Had he been taught self-control in youth, what a difference it would have made!

Though the affection of his uncle and aunt may have helped to spoil the child, it was well they did not insist upon too long hours in the schoolroom, but permitted Tycho plenty of time in

[4] In those days all educated classes, not merely men of learning, had a smattering of Latin.

which to play out-of-doors, think his own thoughts and roam around the lovely countryside surrounding the old Brahe family property of Tostrup. The latent rustle of spring in the air, the trembling tender green of the white birches, the crystal-clear cool lakes, the bluebells and daisies nodding in the sweet breeze, the shallows of the streams gleaming and murmuring across their pebbled beds, cowslips and white anemones gay in their carpeting, damp earthy smells intermingling with their scents .and, amid all this reborn beauty, the intoxicating song of the larks mounting higher and higher into the cool air—this Scania loveliness became part of the boy's youth and remained with him through life.

The University of Copenhagen had been in reality nothing more than a high school, founded by King Christian I when he was in Rome in 1474. It was said it was a penance imposed by the Pope for His Majesty's not understanding Latin and thus being unable to read the Bible. However that may be, the University had languished. In 1537 it had been reestablished according to a plan by the great Bugenhagen, and the charter had been modeled on that of his own university, Wittenberg.

Thirteen being the ripe age for a lad to enter the University,[5] Tycho, with a piped collar around his neck and a small rapier at his side, crossed the Sound from his idyllic home and was delivered by his tutor in April 1559 to the University authorities and the bitter experiences of philosophy, rhetoric and law.

King Frederik had given the University the old palace and grounds of the Catholic bishops. Above its entrance was an eagle, underneath which was written, *Lucem adspicit coelestem* —"He looks up to the light of heaven." No boy who entered the portal was ever to follow the admonition more faithfully.

On his matriculation Tycho was given salt on his tongue as a symbol of wisdom, and water and wine were poured on his head. This done, he was permitted to retire and spit out and clean up before the fourteen University regulations were sol-

[5] Bacon was likewise sent to Cambridge at the age of thirteen.

emnly read to him. In them he was warned against "playing improper games, thieving, loose-living, whoring, breaking in doors, plundering gardens and similar misdemeanors," and was also informed "that if he dishonored a girl, he would be publicly flogged and forced to marry her. If she refused matrimony, he must give her a sufficient sum to make her forget the unfortunate occurrence." The little chap was also given to understand that unruly students were quickly clapped into the cellar jail, and that was where he would land if he preferred drinking and throwing dice to studying the Psalms of David; and further, he was warned that he had better not forget to talk Latin or Greek at meal times.

The curriculum was pretty much all work, conducted entirely in Latin, and little play. There may have been an occasional evening of pleasure, but generally there were endless study hours and a morning start on bread soaked in beer, long before daylight. The boys wore out their breeches on hard benches, and those nearest the porcelain stove were the only ones warm in the icy and foggy winter months.

Niels Hemmingsen was the most renowned of the professors, several times re-elected rector and once was even made vice-chancellor. He was, in addition, the greatest Danish theologian and teacher of his day, and followed the exceptional course of generally lecturing in Danish. A one-time pupil of Melanchthon, during his professorship he published quite a few very popular books in various languages.

Despite one of Hemmingsen's books being entitled *Universalis Daniæ Præceptor*, "Instructor of Entire Denmark," his own and his family's behavior was not always above reproach. An account of the day relates that one Morten Jørgensen accused him "of shamefully reviling his wife before others on the open street," and another report states that his son, Hans, also a professor, "ran around Copenhagen during the night, broke windows with his sword, drank and reeled about intoxicated, bel-

lowed and threatened the life of the municipality's cook." He
had likewise "one evening beaten Morten black and blue when
he found him stark naked in his room, broken the window above
his sick wife's bed and cursed and sworn so that they were at
their wits' end."

Poor Niels' end was a sad one for a distinguished and valued
scholar. Persecution forced him to resign because of his opinions
on the sacraments, and he died at Roskilde a year before his
great pupil and friend Tycho Brahe.

Hemmingsen and his colleagues were most of them a pomp-
ous, didactic lot, laying down the law, much of it correct, but
some of it nonsense. To take just one instance of what they
taught:[6] "Married people must beware of the slyness and swin-
dling propensities of the devil. Angels are, however, on hand
to help married people if they only behave themselves. The first
rule to be observed by a husband is not to run after maids, wid-
ows and harlots; for that is almost as bad as to desire a married
woman.

"The devil knows there is no peace outside wedlock; he has
thus made bishops, monks and priests miserable, writhing crea-
tures, helpless in the face of woman's lures. It is true that Abraham, Isaac and David all had the joy of several wives, but we
must not envy them. As for Solomon, the less we think of his
good fortune the better."

To read the books of, and about, most of the learned men of
this time gives one the impression that outside their own particular subjects they must have been frightful bores.

King Frederik, who realized what hard financial straits
the University was in, came splendidly to the assistance of both
the poor students and the professors, but he also kept an eye
on the latter, as is shown by his letter to the faculty in regard to
the previously mentioned Reverend Morten Jørgensen:

"Receive our good graces.

[6] Niels Hemmingsen, *Om Ægteskab*. København, 1562.

"Let it be known that it has come to our knowledge how a certain Herr Morten Jørgensen, who has previously served in a sacred home of refuge, not only has led a strange life of gluttony and drunkenness but also has permitted and arranged drinking bouts in his house whereby he and his wife have given cause for much lewdness and adultery, and though he has often been reminded by both priests and others not to permit such things in his house, this has been of no avail, and as it is unworthy of a clergyman thus to give cause for the wrath of God, let it be known that Morten has also put up scandalous writings in various parts of the town and in them shown himself rebellious, and allowed himself disobedience against his superiors; therefore, we wish that he and his wife be expelled immediately not only from the town of Copenhagen but from the diocese of Sjælland. . . . Thereby our will is done."

By the statute of 1539, chairs were created for fourteen professors, three of divinity, one of law, two of medicine and eight of the faculty of arts. The latter taught courses in rhetoric and philosophy that included much that had nothing whatever to do with these subjects.

To encourage learning in the University, Frederik II issued a proclamation ordering the burgomaster and aldermen of his good city of Copenhagen to refrain from offending the professors or curtailing their privileges and liberties. He likewise provided scholarships for a hundred poor students, stipulating that the beneficiaries must never forget to speak Latin at meals. As previously mentioned, the Catholic clergy had been forced to disgorge their rich revenues and fat lands, representing some thirty per cent of the country's finest acreage, so after generations of chronic bankruptcy and borrowing from the Jews, the Crown had money with which to support worthy causes like the University, and also decidedly unworthy ones, such as wars with neighboring states.

Most of Tycho's fellow pupils were poor, as evidenced by a rhyme of the day:

Rich students eat the King's fare;
Poor students are both hungry and bare.[7]

Many of them were so poor that they were obliged to walk the streets, hoping to earn a few extra coppers by singing on the doorsteps of the more prosperous citizens.

There were two groups of students, those whose parents wished their sons later to receive a further smattering of knowledge than that which the University had afforded, in order to fit them better for their careers in the service of the Crown, and then the majority, poorer boys who were to enter the ministry, medicine, law or one of the other professions. The first group almost invariably turned to Germany for their higher education, where they generally were sent in the care of tutors to Wittenberg, Rostock, Tübingen, Heidelberg or Leipzig, and also at times to Basel, Paris or Montpellier. Some of these universities were fully comparable in what they taught to Oxford or Cambridge, Paris, Salamanca, Leyden, Padua or Bologna. Rostock being nearest to home, most of them naturally went there. Wherever they were sent, Latin was exclusively the university language.

During the years 1559 to 1562, Tycho, the boy from Scania, stood out among the University youngsters, owing to his eager curiosity, intelligence and ability. Unfortunately his courses in law did not, towards the end of his academic career, seem to interest him particularly. He was, however, highly excited when he heard his masters discussing the total eclipse of the sun predicted for August 21, 1560. His principal early biographer, the seventeenth century sage Gassendi, states that to Tycho the eclipse "seemed something divine, for how could men know the motions of the stars so accurately that they could, long before, foretell their places and relative position? How was such a thing possible, wondered the young lad. It was miraculous. How could they know? What science provided such knowledge of the

[7] *De rige studenter æde Kongens kost;*
De fattige lide baade hunger og frost.

[19]

future, if true? If astronomy, then this must be divine and far more worthy of attention than what he was learning daily."

The great day of the expected eclipse arrived, bright and clear. Tycho Brahe saw and believed. The spark was lit.

The professor of mathematics and also the professor of medicine, to whom the lad turned, were rather at a loss to answer his persistent astronomical questions. They did not wish to lead him along such bypaths away from his prescribed studies, and probably themselves did not know the answers to many of his questions. To turn him off, they advised him to try to obtain the *Ephemerides* by Johann Stadius and Ptolemy's works,[8] to be had in Latin. This Tycho did the moment he had accumulated the spare pennies, with the result that he spent far more time poring over his purchases than over his philosophy and rhetoric, which bored him in comparison with the system of the cosmos and the course of the planets. A new world was opening for the boy, one that fascinated him and held him spellbound.

Now commenced, at first tentatively and with some bewilderment, that ceaseless searching for truth which was to continue unabated for forty years. What people said, what he read in books, did not satisfy Tycho. He received no adequate answers to the great questions. He was never to look the full truth in the face, but what he eventually did was to lead a great science along a new path, and what he accomplished was to enable his assistant to reveal it in its full beauty.

Tycho differed from most students of his day who went abroad to receive an exterior polish, to acquire foreign impressions and languages, to see the sights and learn how to associate with foreigners. He looked across the frontiers for more knowledge to help him answer the questions that the study of the stars had already put into his head.

At the beginning of the year 1562 he had finished his course in Copenhagen, and the time had come for him to continue his

---

[8] Ptolemy's *Almagest* was the only printed book on astronomy of the day. Tycho purchased the Basel edition of 1551 for two precious Joachimsthaler.

study of law in Germany. Considerable correspondence had taken place on the matter between his uncle and the University authorities, both as to where he would best be sent and in whose care. Tycho was as yet not quite sixteen. Prague, Heidelberg, Leipzig and Wittenberg were all considered; each one had something to recommend it. Weighing the pros and cons, his advisers finally decided on Leipzig.

A young, sober and brilliant student, not quite twenty, by the name of Anders Sørensen Vedel,[9] the son of a respected Vejle citizen, was selected to accompany Tycho as his private tutor, in the hope that he might arrest the boy's scientific inclinations. Here too the choice was a fortunate one. Vedel had not the independent means for foreign study, but being only a little more than four years older than Tycho, he might prove a companion as well as an adviser and guardian or *Hovmester*, as the term was in those days. Though strained relations were bound to arise from Tycho's desertion of the profession chosen for him, their friendship outlasted these difficulties and remained steadfast throughout their lives. After they had parted, each to go his different way, Vedel became a well-known figure, serving first as court preacher and then as royal historian,[10] and Queen Sophia, the wife of Frederik II, became his devoted admirer.

[9] Andreas Severinus Velleius Cimber, in the Latin form. Cimber indicates his Jutland origin.

[10] Influenced by the humanistic tendencies of his age, Vedel later in life turned to many interesting tasks, the greatest of which was undertaken at the instigation of Chancellor Friis, namely, thirty years of laborious translation into Danish of the most important work in Latin by a Dane up to his time, the *Chronicle of Saxo Grammaticus*. So as to procure for his friend the paper on which to print it, Tycho made a public appeal for rag contributions "in order that the deeds of our ancestors be not buried in oblivion." Vedel settled in the little Jutland town of Ribe as a member of the cathedral chapter, where he devoted himself to the most congenial task of writing a comprehensive Danish history.

Nevertheless, Vedel not only lost his honorable appointment at Ribe to another scholar, Dr. Krag, who had more friends at court, but was cruelly forced to give up for the benefit of his successor all the valuable historical information he had collected on his travels throughout many years. He was thus, to his considerable chagrin, relieved of further work on the history, but he continued research among old songs and published *A Hundred Ballads about Kings, Giants and Others*. It was in a way a fortunate diversion of his talents, for the history could be continued by others who probably would not have had the taste or acumen to discover the fine old ballads. He did quite a little publishing, and was a jolly fellow, liked by

The two students arrived in Leipzig in March 1562, and when they had found pleasant lodgings in the house of the professor of jurisprudence, Tycho matriculated in the University, famous for its law school and its professor, the famous humanist, Joachim Camerarius. How was Tycho now to pursue his astronomical studies without getting into trouble with Vedel, and how might he best equip himself for his dual role of law student and stargazer? There seemed only one way: to attend the boring law lectures and study legal subjects during the daytime when his tutor's sharp eye was upon him, and to gaze at the heavens on clear nights when Vedel was asleep.[11]

> Night after night, among the gabled roofs,
> Climbing and creeping through a world unknown
> Save to the roosting stork, he learned to find
> The constellations, Cassiopeia's throne,
> The Plough still pointing to the Polar Star,
> The Sword-belt of Orion. There he watched
> The movements of the planets, hours and hours,
> And wondered at the mystery of it all.[12]

This Tycho not only did, but continued to do for a long time without arousing any suspicion that he was burning the candle at both ends. He must have enjoyed astonishingly good health to accomplish what he had set himself to do. From Ptolemy's books he learned how to use the Ptolemaic tables, but he soon realized the immediate necessity of a far greater knowledge of higher mathematics than he possessed. Fortunately, the un-

all, but had, alas, been born, as was said by a friend, "under a contrary [*knarvurren*] planet."

The only sidelight we have on Vedel's family life recounts his somewhat original method of educating his children. Wishing to make them thoroughly understand the sufferings of the Saviour on Good Friday, he spent a good part of it every year thrashing his sons and daughters. Evidently he took his parental obligations very seriously.

[11] His first registered observation was taken in August 1563, the year of the outbreak of the disastrous Seven Years War with Sweden.

[12] Alfred Noyes, *The Torch Bearers*, Vol. I, "Watchers of the Sky." J. B. Lippincott & Co., Philadelphia, Pa.

suspecting Vedel did not demur at his pupil's laudable ambition for greater knowledge in this science, though it did not exactly lead to a mastery of jurisprudence. He did warn him, however, that a recent Copenhagen teacher of mathematics by the name of Ejler Hansen had become insane from overindulgence in mathematics. The warning had no effect.

On making discreet inquiries as to the best teacher in mathematics, Tycho found to his disappointment that the famous mathematician, Professor Johannes Homelius, had died. But his successors and former pupils, Bartholomæus Scultetus (Schultz) and Valentin Thau, replaced him well, and to them Tycho frankly explained his passion and his difficulties. They sympathized with the lad, advised him what preliminary books to purchase and, what was more, offered to aid him, later on, in procuring simple, inexpensive instruments. Books and instruments—how was he to purchase them when he had to give Vedel a strict accounting of all he spent? There was only one way, and that was to scrape together and save up all the small sums doled out to him for simple pleasures and an occasional evening with his friends.

Little by little the books were purchased, and a small globe obtained, about the size of an orange. By comparing the stars with those depicted on the globe, Tycho succeeded in a month's time in becoming acquainted with the constellations visible above the horizon at Leipzig at that time of year. He gave Scultetus, who had now become a friend, a wooden radius, begging him to divide it in the manner adopted by the great Homalius. The radius was returned to him marked as desired. He went on making his nightly observations out of his study window and on his little globe he marked as accurately as he was able whatever he had seen.

Next Tycho purchased the *Tabulæ Bergensis* and started eagerly on the study of the planetary motions. By the use of the *Ephemerides* of Stadius he learned to distinguish the planets and also came to the astonishing conclusion that the *Ephemeri-*

des were inaccurate. Having obtained the Alphonsine and Prussian[13] tables and having compared them with his own calculations and observations, Tycho observed great differences in the results, finding the Alphonsine tables a month out, and the Prussian also several days in error. And so in his youthful enthusiasm he decided forthwith to devote his life to the accurate construction of tables, which he believed were the basis of astronomy.

J. L. E. Dreyer, an outstanding biographer of Tycho, says: "His equipment now consisted, outside his astronomical and mathematical books, of his little globe, of a pair of compasses and a radius or 'cross staff.' This consisted of a light, graduated rod about three feet long and another rod about half that length, also graduated, which at the center could slide along the longer one, so that they formed a right angle. The instrument could be used in two ways. Two sights might be fixed at the ends of the shorter rod, and one at the end of the longer rod, and the observer, having placed the latter close to his eye, moved the cross rod along until he saw through its two sights the two objects of which he wanted to measure the angular distance. Or, one of the sights of the shorter arm might be movable, and the observer first arbitrarily placed the shorter arm at any of the graduations on the longer one, and then shifted the movable sight along until he saw the two objects through it and a sight fixed at the center of the transversal arm. In either case the graduations and a table of tangents furnished the required angle."[14]

Tycho used his compasses by placing their center close to one of his eyes and pointing the two legs to two stars or to a planet and a star, thus finding the angular distances, afterwards applying the compasses to a circle drawn on paper and divided into degrees and half-degrees.

[13] The *Tabulæ Prutenicæ* were prepared in 1551 by Erasmus Reinhold at the expense of Duke Albert of Prussia, and were calculated on the basis of the Copernican theory.

[14] J. L. E. Dreyer, *Tycho Brahe.* Edinburgh, 1890.

Such were the pathetically crude instruments with which the lad's genius broke through ignorance and superstition and by which his eminently practical talent surmounted all obstacles. He made his last observations only a few years before Galileo announced his great discovery of the telescope. What Tycho accomplished without it, without logarithms or even a pendulum clock, remains almost unbelievable.

Tycho's nightly experiences and his recording of his observations left his mind seething with confused knowledge. His attempts to acquire greater clarity by reading only added to his intellectual excitement. How much was truth; what was ignorance, and what was merely superstition?

The confusion of astronomy and astrology was only one of the many problems that bewildered Tycho. Since the time of the ancients, astrology or the art of predicting coming events, and particularly the fortunes of men, from planetary positions, had been closely bound up with astronomy. By the sixteenth century, with its presses and many yearly calendars filled with prognostics, astrology had become so universally recognized that astrologers were held in high repute and found employment in the households of the great.[15] Throughout the Renaissance, astrology remained respectable, and Tycho's great contemporary, Galileo, cast horoscopes at the court of the Medici.[16]

As a child of his age, Tycho naturally shared with other astronomers the belief that it was possible to foretell the future from the stars, and that there must be some connection between their movements and the course of events in the lives of men. However, his belief in most of the hocus-pocus of astrology weakened year by year, and when he was later commanded to cast horoscopes, he did so with considerable misgiving. Tycho never felt himself on solid ground without scientific proof be-

[15] His greatest pupil, Johann Kepler, averred half humorously, half indignantly, that the astronomer could only support himself by ministering to the follies of astronomy's "silly little daughter," astrology.

[16] Few doctors would have thought of curing a fever unless they knew at what hour it had begun and how that hour coincided with the constellation of the patient.

[25]

hind him, but at the age of sixteen or seventeen, all he could reason was that some predictions, like that of the eclipse in Copenhagen, came true, while others evidently did not.

If astrology did not seem to Tycho the complete absurdity that it does to most of us, it was partly because to him and his contemporaries the universe had very narrow limits. That he, even as a boy, dared doubt the astrological beliefs of his day shows remarkable intellectual courage. Even the great Melanchthon lectured at Wittenberg on the reading of the stars. The Valois and the Medici and many others in power and authority in his time turned to their astrologers for advice in the most critical moments of their lives and were guided by what they advised. Charles V took a vital interest in astrological predictions and so did Louise of Savoy, the mother of Francis I. Catherine de Medici had the greatest faith, first in Cosimo Ruggieri and later in Michel Nôtredame (Nostradamus); Henry II sent for the famous astrologer Larivière to come to the court; and when Anne of Austria gave birth to Louis XIV, she had her astrologer Morin hidden behind the tapestry so he might the better cast a reliable horoscope. In Tycho's own sixteenth century, astrology as a university subject was not quite as much studied as during the two previous centuries, but chairs for its teaching still existed at Bologna and Padua.

Tycho was informed by the wise and learned that each planet ruled some special part of the world and of the human body, so that according to its position it might induce certain conditions in the countries under its influence and cause or divert certain diseases. Again, he was told that certain persons born under particular planets were believed to be endowed with temperamental characteristics corresponding to the supposed nature of the planet.[17] "How," he remarked one day, "when we see that animals and plants, metals and minerals have their use and

[17] From this belief came such terms as "mercurial," "jovial" and "saturnine"; words like "ill-starred" and "ascendancy" are also relics of the once universal belief.

importance, can we then believe that the heavenly bodies should be created without their purposes?"

So Tycho naturally studied astrology and was occupied practically with its pursuits and at times even misled by its delusions. In later days, however, he was to carry on his astronomical labors with his mind free from superstition, despising the knavery and vanity of astrologers.

A further matter of the greatest importance and confusion to Tycho was the acceptance by many scholars of the Copernican system, which tended to destroy the older beliefs. The wise Scultetus could merely shake his head when Tycho went to him for guidance in the matter. So, for the time being, Ptolemy and the tables he had purchased were the only lights upon his path.

The Alphonsine tables had appeared in 1252, and the Prussian, calculated on the Copernican principles, in 1551, only twelve years before they fell into Tycho's hands. Although they represented celestial movements far better than did those of the thirteenth century, they were full of the discrepancies to be discovered and corrected a few years later by Tycho and the distinguished landgrave William IV of Hesse-Cassel, who was to become a close friend of Tycho's. More exact observations were in turn to prompt a reform of methods.

From Claudius Ptolemy, the Alexandrian Greek astronomer who lived about A.D. 130 and whose work was still a complete compendium of the astronomy of the day, the young enthusiast more than fourteen centuries later learned that he lived in a spherical, stationary world, around which moved, in circular orbits of their own, the sun, the moon and the planets.[18] Each planet moved in general slowly around the earth, while the whole system whirled around westward each twenty-four hours. This seemed to Tycho perfectly logical, for he reasoned that if

[18] Tycho's precious copy of Ptolemy, which he had purchased in Copenhagen in 1560, remained, at least prior to the Second World War, one of the chief treasures of the library of the University of Prague, copiously annotated and marked by the young student at Leipzig.

the world itself rotated and a stone were let fall from, say, a high tower, it would reach the earth at a distance away from the foot of the tower. As it did not, his own world must stand still and Ptolemy must be right.

Then one day Tycho's speculations and nocturnal observations were rudely interrupted. Vedel, having for some time suspected the surreptitious activities of his young charge, had finally gotten ample proof of what was going on. He faced him with his iniquity and hard words passed between the two. Vedel must have recognized the boy's stubborn determination to continue with his stargazing at the expense of fitting himself for the career for which he was intended, and sensed the passion was one that might be impossible to quench, for he took his time in writing home to his patron, Tycho's uncle.

While Vedel was weighing the dilemma, Tycho received a letter, in 1565, from Jørgen Brahe, instructing tutor and charge to return home, for he wished to see the boy before taking command as vice-admiral of a squadron of the Danish fleet under the great Herluf Trolle. The northern Seven Years' War between Frederik II and Erik XIV of Sweden[19] had already been going on for five years, and the uncle was about to leave for his flagship. Another of his uncles, Steen Bille, was also leaving as a colonel with his six companies for the Swedish front. Tycho packed up with a heavy heart, for he felt that all his hopes might be shattered when he was once more in Denmark, under his uncle's watchful eye. He left with the happy conviction, however, that his greatest Leipzig experience had been the conjunction of Jupiter and Saturn that he had observed in 1563.

Tycho and Vedel shook hands, forgetting their recent differences, and headed home by way of Wittenberg. But uncle and nephew were not destined to remain together long, for an accident put an end to Jørgen Brahe's life shortly after Tycho's arrival. King Frederik, accompanied by some of his courtiers, was

---

[19] A French contemporary stated: "The Danes and Swedes hate each other as much as cats and dogs or English and French."

passing over a rather rickety bridge leading from Copenhagen to the adjacent island of Amager, when his horse took fright at something and plunged with its rider into the water. Jørgen Brahe immediately jumped his horse in after his floundering master and succeeded in extricating him as well as himself. But while the king escaped with a wetting, Brahe caught pneumonia and died.

Through this accident, Tycho, now nineteen years old, had by his sudden inheritance become independent. On the other hand, his uncle's death affected him greatly, for Jørgen had shown him nothing but kindness and affection as long as he could remember, and his future career and happiness had been one of his uncle's great concerns. Though his aunt made him doubly welcome back at Tostrup, where she now was alone, he felt the urge to return to Germany and the work to which he was now free to devote himself. He finally decided to turn with his doubts to his mother's understanding brother, Steen Bille *til* Vandaas og Raabeløb, and open his whole heart to him. This high-minded gentleman had always shown sympathy for his nephew's scientific research, instead of taking the narrow, big-oted point of view assumed by all the rest of his family and associates.

Tycho was not disillusioned. His Uncle Steen entered with interest into his plans, advising Tycho, however, first to spend a year at home looking after the property that his Uncle Jørgen had left him, to present himself at court and, at least temporarily, assume the position that was rightfully his as one of the first noblemen of the realm.

His Uncle Steen evidently appealed to him in just the right way, for instead of balking, as might have been expected of one of his temperament, he decided to take the good advice offered. While he enjoyed being back in Scania, he was infuriated, when in Copenhagen, by the wild, arrogant young noblemen who spent all their time drinking, gambling and quarreling, and who sneered at and cold-shouldered him. He stood it as long as he could, but in the summer of 1566 the wish to return to his work became too strong for him to resist. When we consider the situation, it is above all praise that he should have had the steadfast determination and courage to pursue his aim, surmount all the prejudices of his time and class and devote himself to his science despite the scorn, abuse and ridicule to which he was subjected. He was indeed fired by an urge that nothing could arrest.

He wrote a friend, "Neither my country nor my friends keep me back. One who has courage finds a home in every place and lives a happy life everywhere. Friends, too, one can find in all countries. There will always be time enough to return to the cold North to follow the general example, and, like the rest, to play in pride and luxury for the rest of one's years with wine, dogs and horses. May God, as I trust He will, grant me a better lot."

CHAPTER THREE

Look unto the heavens, and see.—
Job 35:5

YCHO'S first thought was naturally to return to Leipzig, to be with his old friends and teachers. There were, indeed, many attractions in that delightful city. There was the great booksellers' mart to which the best publishers, generally learned men, came from all over Europe with their latest editions and bindings, and where he now was free to purchase without giving any accounting. There were the famous New Year's, Easter and Michaelmas fairs, with their offerings, and the new Rathaus with its excellent cellar in which he might endlessly discuss mathematical and astronomical problems with his seniors.

Despite the fact that it had lost reputation among many, owing to certain Calvinistic tendencies, Wittenberg seemed to him preferable, however. It was a common gathering place for Danish students, had splendid teachers in mathematics and was in close touch with Denmark. Luther's and Melanchthon's powerful, rebellious spirits still seemed to hover over the place. There had been the cradle of the Reformation; there they had taught; there Luther had burned the Papal bull and nailed on the church door his ninety-five theses against the doctrine of church indulgences. The elector, Frederik the Wise, as late as 1502 had founded the University, which, due to its splendid teachers, had rapidly risen to prominence and renown. Frederik had endowed two chairs in mathematics, thereby emphasizing the importance of the subject.

So there Tycho went and settled down to work under Kaspar Peucer, a distinguished historian and professor of medicine, astronomy and mathematics, and physician to the Elector of Saxony. Strange to say, the three subjects were then supposed to be intimately connected and branches of the same science. Tycho's stay was short, but the eclipse of the moon that took place on October 28, 1566 made it especially memorable to him.

Before he had been there many months, to his dismay plague and pestilence broke out in the city. As several students had already died and the wealthier burghers were fleeing with their families to healthier surroundings, Tycho found that the only sensible thing to do was to follow their example and leave Wittenberg as soon as possible.

The way home lay through Rostock, where he decided to stop sufficiently long to make the acquaintance of Professor Heinrich Brucæus and also to see Professor David Chytræus, who had cared for many Danish students in a fatherly manner. He wanted also to see what Rostock's University had to offer and to make the acquaintance of some of its scholars. To meet scholars, particularly those interested in his own science, became and remained throughout his life of the greatest importance to Tycho. As he grew older and more and more celebrated, if he did not know personally most of the scholars in his own field, he at least corresponded with a large number of those in England, the Low Countries, Germany, France and Italy.

Among his countrymen matriculated in the University of Rostock was a nobleman like himself, named Manderup Parsbjerg. He was later to rise in the king's service, to become a privy councilor and even chancellor and, strange to say, to sit in judgment on one of Tycho's future misdemeanors. Tycho and Parsbjerg met at Professor Bachmeister's house, where there was a good deal of celebration in honor of the engagement of the professor's daughter. It was not a girl, however, but disagreement on some mathematical point that caused so serious a quarrel between the two of them that mutual friends had to separate them. Unfortunately they met again a week later at a Christmas party where beer and wine, added to mathematical difficulties, started trouble anew between the two young gamecocks. This time there was no separating them. They left the Christmas celebrations, adjourned to a secluded spot beside a graveyard, "shrouded in complete darkness," and drew their swords. After a very short fight young Parsbjerg cut off a good slice of Tycho's nose.[1] This conclusively ended the dispute. Medical science had unfortunately not arrived at a point where it knew how to graft the nose on again. A contemporary, commenting on the unfortunate incident, says: "As Tycho was not used to going around without a nose, and did not like to, he went to the expense of purchasing a new one. He was not satisfied, as some others might have been, to put on a wax one, but, being a nobleman of wealth, ordered a nose made of gold and silver so soberly painted and adjusted that it seemed of a natural appearance."

A certain Wilhelm Janson, who saw Tycho frequently during one period of his life, says that he always had a little box in his pocket, filled with glue or salve that he applied whenever the nose became wobbly. Another of Tycho's companions surmises that: "The nose question may conceivably have had something to do with the selection of the humble life-companion he later took, as a lady of the court and his own class might well have demurred at marrying a noseless husband."

Rostock was the most important city in Mecklenburg-Schwerin and was, remaining so for some time, a member of the Hanseatic League, ranking next to Lübeck among the Baltic cities. Tycho found it stimulating and would willingly have remained longer. While there, however, he committed a second folly, though not quite so great as that which caused him to pay for a mathematical opinion with his nose. He put his knowledge of astrology to the test in casting the horoscope of Sultan Suleiman. He had posted up in the University some Latin verses announcing that the recent lunar eclipse foretold the Sultan's death, and only learned later that that event had actually taken place long before he prophesied it.

Having surmounted the excitement of the loss of part of his nose as well as that of a great eclipse of the sun, which he now

[1] Upon Tycho's death Parsbjerg wrote generously of him, stating how much he regretted having done him the injury and complaining of its having been referred to in his former opponent's funeral oration.

[35]

was able to study as a real student of astronomy and not merely as a curious boy, he went back to Denmark for a short stay during the summer of 1567. There he found that his Uncle Steen Bille and his Uncle Jørgen's wife, Inger Oxe, had pleaded his cause at court to good advantage. Inger was a sister of the influential chancellor, Peder Oxe, and as he was extremely fond of her, whenever on a rare occasion she asked a favor, Oxe generally granted it. This time she begged, seconded by Steen Bille, the promise of the first vacant canonry in Roskilde cathedral for Tycho Brahe. King Frederik agreed to this in a formal, written statement, and as some of the canons were old and liable to pass on shortly, it was only a question of a bit of a wait before Tycho would fall heir to a profitable sinecure. But he could not remain still. Even with this chance awaiting him, the wanderlust once more overtook him, and 1568 saw him again in Wittenberg. From there he continued to Augsburg, where he made what was to prove the most important of his many stays in Germany.

The free city of Augsburg was one of the most flourishing cities in Europe, prominent in commerce, manufacture and the arts. Together with Nuremberg, it was an emporium of trade between northern and southern Europe, and its merchants were princes whose ships sailed the seven seas. The greatest of these, the Fuggers, possessed a library in which Tycho had longed to work. Beyond this, however, his principal interest was to engage the skillful Augsburg instrument workers, probably the first in Europe, to make him such instruments as he felt he needed imperatively in order to do accurate work, and which he now was in a position to afford. Among these, the most important for his work, he felt, were a quadrant, a sextant and a globe.

His rising fame had preceded him, and shortly after his arrival he was fortunate enough to gain the friendship of the brothers Johannes Baptista and Paul Hainzel, one the burgomaster, the other an alderman of the city. During the two years of his stay (1569-1571) these two prominent citizens opened

Tycho's Great Quadrant

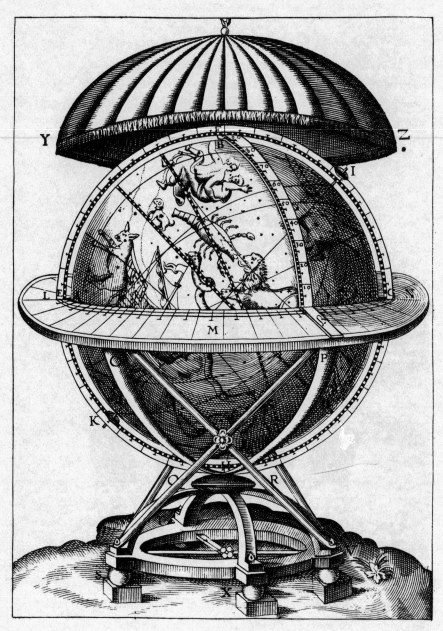

Tycho's Famous Five-Foot Globe

all doors to Tycho and entered enthusiastically into whatever he undertook.

He commenced by regulating his days between superintending and advising in the workshops and studying chemistry. The beauty and splendor of the imperial city, which so recently had been the center of such momentous events, fairly dazzled the young Dane. Here it was that Charles V had come to face the Protestant storm. The love of the arts that filled its wealthy citizens was an eye opener to the Copenhagen student. Though he was not exactly a modest young man, nevertheless it surprised as much as it pleased him upon arriving in the city to have one celebrated savant after another brought to his lodgings to meet "the great Danish astronomer."

With the advice of the Hainzels and the mathematician and humanist, Hieronymus Wolf, Tycho turned to the most cunning artisans to replace his earlier, somewhat primitive, quadrant, ordering one that was clearly divided into the single minutes of a degree. The projected instrument finally evolved into one of 14-cubit[2] radius. Tycho was a bit dismayed when, during the progress of its execution, he realized how much it would cost, but the good burgomaster said he would gladly shoulder a generous share of the expense in order that his eminent friend might have the needed tools. So many of the best craftsmen, jewelers, smiths and carpenters were busied in its manufacture that it was completed in a month, and twenty proud artisans, followed by a jubilant, cheering throng, carried it to the garden of Paul Hainzel's country seat at Göggingen, about a mile outside of Augsburg, where it was temporarily set up and employed in measuring heights.

As this quadrant was only fitted to determine altitudes of celestial bodies, Tycho decided to construct a large sextant for the purpose of measuring angular distances of the stars. This was

[2] About 19 feet, its entire height measuring almost 37 feet. (Harald Mortensen of Copenhagen in a description of the quadrant.)

likewise done, and it became of constant use to him and his friends during his stay.

Tycho's principal astronomical work in Augsburg was the examination of the apparent movement of the planets and the fixed stars. As a basis for this, accurate data of their relative positions became requisite. For this purpose he decided to order the manufacture of a huge five-foot globe on which he could place all the fixed stars whose positions had been determined by his observations. It was to be as close to a perfect sphere as art and science could make it, and to be covered with sheet brass, invisibly soldered, on which he proposed, wherever his own observatory might be, to engrave the place of every star and planet as exactly as he could determine it.

This globe was to prove a journal of Tycho's life and embody most of his observations, and become the most famous of all his instruments, known throughout the length and breadth of Europe. He had it sent to him from his observatory at Hveen when he was in Prague during the last years of his life, and upon his death it was sold by his descendants with his other instruments to Emperor Rudolph, who made partial payment for them. During the Thirty Years' War, Christian IV's son, Ulrik, whose horoscope Tycho had cast, came across it in a Jesuit convent in Silesia and shipped it home by Skipper Mikkelsen from Stralsund. The professors of the University of Copenhagen rejoiced to have it back and set it up in their observatory on top of the Round Tower, where unfortunately it was burned in 1728.

Tycho worked hard and the men he met in Augsburg widened his horizon immeasurably. He was no longer a Danish astronomer, but a European one. One of the most remarkable men of his age, the Huguenot Petrus Ramus of Paris (Pierre de la Ramee),[3] who had been forced to leave his home, came in contact with Tycho at this time and influenced him greatly in giving him a more liberal view of astrology and a deeper insight into the importance of astronomy. While the distinguished

[3] Humanist and mathematician who perished in the massacre of St. Bartholomew.

French philosopher disagreed with Tycho on certain points, they were both intent upon seeing the science of astronomy renovated by new and accurate observations, in order that true explanations of the celestial motions might be attempted. They both felt the necessity of replacing the old, speculative study of nature by independent, accurate observation as the basis of all the sciences.

Once more Tycho was called home, and this time it was by news of his father's serious illness. The elder Brahe died on May 9, 1571,[4] and Tycho and his brother Steen inherited the joint lordship of Knudstrup. For the time being Tycho, the elder of the two, on whom the administration of the property largely rested, would have to spend most of his time in Scania. Once more his uncle Steen Bille understood the situation and dealt wisely with it. He realized the lad's intellectual and social loneliness both at home and in Copenhagen, and the absolute necessity for him to be engaged in matters that interested him. Tycho had on his return recounted enthusiastically to him all the chemical work he had been doing in Augsburg. So the uncle suggested that, instead of moving into lonely Knudstrup, Tycho come to live with him on his nearby property, the Cistercian Abbey of Herrevad, founded by Archbishop Eskild in 1144. Steen Bille had been told "to go and live in the Abbey, because ungodly living was going on there"; the abbot might remain, but Bille was charged to see that he behaved himself. Steen suggested to Tycho that they jointly install a fine chemical laboratory in one of the Abbey's suitable farm buildings, and this proved the very bait with which to catch Tycho and make him temporarily abandon the thought of returning south.

The uncle soon noticed how much his young nephew had altered since he last saw him. He seemed to have shaken off a good deal of the narrow, stifling atmosphere of the little home

---

[4] In a very moving letter of May 18, 1571, to his old tutor, Anders Sørensen Vedel, Tycho describes the serenity of his father's death in spite of great pain. He says: "We have not lived well until we have shown we can die well."

circle. His horizon had broadened in every way; he felt singularly confident of himself and his own powers, and could not help looking down upon the petty concerns of his Copenhagen contemporaries; while with some of the older, wiser heads, like his good friends from university days, Johannes Pratensis[5] and Hans Frandsen of Ribe, professor of medicine, he kept in constant touch by correspondence, or visits whenever possible.

The fact is that Tycho had come home a man with a European reputation, which his genius had earned him at an unusually early age. Johann Kepler, the greatest of his pupils, who was one day to equal his master, and was consequently a competent judge, wrote of him: "The restoration of astronomy was by that phoenix of astronomers, Tycho, first conceived and determined in the year 1564." Thus at the age of seventeen Tycho had had the temerity to disagree on cardinal points with all former astronomers, and his ambition was, during his twenties, to create a new epoch in astronomy as a science of observation.

Not only did his uncle promise to install a chemical laboratory at Herrevad, where, in addition to much experimentation and distilling, the everlasting search for gold was to be prosecuted, but Steen Bille even agreed to arrange quarters for a miniature observatory. Its first installation was the precious Augsburg sextant. His uncle was himself genuinely interested, in an amateurish manner, in the various chemical experiments going on in the laboratory and would often spend hours there watching his nephew. Jointly they devised a paper mill and a glass-making plant, which were the first of their kind in Scandinavia. Tycho, of course, furnished the brains and his Uncle Steen the funds, and the king, to whom the latter wrote, was asked to supply the badly needed paper-maker. Strange to say, not a single astronomical observation is to be found among Tycho's many papers remaining to us from this period, that is, from the year 1570 to November 1572.

---

[5] A monument to Pratensis was on his death erected in Our Lady's Church in Copenhagen with an inscription by Tycho.

On the evening of November 11, 1572, as Tycho was coming back from the laboratory to the main Abbey building, he was startled by seeing an exceedingly bright new star in the constellation of Cassiopeia. He stopped short in astonishment. Among the wonders he had already witnessed had been the eclipse of the sun during his Copenhagen student days, the conjunction of Jupiter and Saturn in 1563, and a remarkable eclipse of the sun in the summer of 1567, but here, if he could believe his eyes, was something even more marvelous. He stopped servants and peasants, loitering on the way home, and asked them, "Do you see it? What does it look like to you?" They all verified that there, where he pointed, was certainly a very brilliant star, though of course they had never noticed whether it had been there before. Trembling with excitement, oblivious of the waiting supper, Tycho rushed for his Augsburg sextant, measured the distance of the star from the nine principal, well-known stars in Cassiopeia and made hurried notes as to its magnitude, color and other characteristics. His mind was awhirl with excitement. Was it a fixed star? Was it a comet? It was certainly more brilliant than Sirius, probably equal to Venus in all her glory when nearest to the earth. Having accomplished all that was possible for the time being, he rushed to inform his uncle of the great event, "with the gusto of a father announcing the birth of his first-born."

The star remained visible until March 1574, that is, for seventeen months, and we may be sure that during this time Tycho gazed at it as a lover would at his sweetheart. He definitely determined that it was fixed, that it had no parallax and that in every respect it seemed like an ordinary star. "The star was at first like Venus and Jupiter," he wrote, "and its immediate effect will therefore be pleasant, but since it became like Mars, there will next come a period of wars, seditions, captivity, death of princes[6] and destruction of cities, together with dryness and fiery meteors in the air, pestilence and venomous snakes. Lastly

[6] The massacre of the night of St. Bartholomew occurred on August 25, 1573.

the star became like Saturn, and there will therefore finally come a time of want, death and imprisonment, and all kinds of sad things." And again, "Its brilliance surpassed that of Sirius, Vega or Jupiter, and persons with sharp eyes could see the star in the daytime, yes, in the very middle of the day, if it was clear."

Now the chemical laboratory became sadly neglected, for, when not gazing at the star, Tycho was writing about it. On rare occasions his uncle would force him into accompanying him to Copenhagen, where the capital's artisans, with the assistance of Pratensis, were making Tycho another copper globe, more modest in proportion than the Augsburg one, as well as other instruments. While he was there, Tycho and Pratensis seldom failed to put their heads together. Then there were court functions from which he would steal off to talk about the star with his learned friends. When he first gave the news to Pratensis and Charles Dancey, the French envoy to the Danish court, they would not believe him until he had taken them to the rooftop and pointed the star out to them.

At court, it was the same old story—ridicule of the work on which he was frittering away his time. One of the fops, Tage Krabbe, was one day making fun of Tycho. As Tage approached him he remarked: "Why, here we have the cynical Diogenes!"

"How do you make that out?" asked Tycho.

"You are buried in your nonsense," replied Tage, "just as Diogenes was in his tub."

"Oh, I wouldn't compare you to such a little fellow," said Tycho. "No, you remind me of Julius Caesar."

"And just how?"

"Caesar preferred to be the first in any other city rather than second in Rome," retorted Tycho, "and you would rather be first among fools than the second or third among the learned."

Tycho's attitude towards these ignorant critics is indicated in a letter that he wrote to a friend at this time: "Neither their laughter nor their intrigues frighten me away from my celestial observations. Let some of them pride themselves on their victories and prate loudly and recount their descent from earliest time, or endeavor to benefit by the deeds of their forefathers. Let others, devoured by stinginess or ambition, concern themselves about royal and princely favor, riches, possessions and great orders. Let some amuse themselves drinking and swilling day upon day, and some in amours and love's adventures. Let some who wish to waste their time and money amuse themselves with cards and dice, and others by hunting stags and hares. Let those who think it fine ride and cavort on their horses, and let others amuse themselves in such manner as they think noblemen should, for by such exercise noble deeds are tested, and nobility possibly demands noble actions. I do not envy them such, but regret that those who possess excellence which might benefit others should desire such things.[7] I must however confess that this [horsemanship] may at times have its uses, for it benefits the body, if done with moderation. Yes, I myself and others may at times do likewise, for I do not think it requires great skill. And though I myself bear the name of a distinguished, noble race and am born a Brahe, and on the maternal side come from the ancient Billes, this does not affect me. For what I myself have not personally accomplished, but have received by descent and ancestry, I would not count my own. My mind is set on much greater things, in which there is real work. Happy is he, here on earth, who places heaven above the earth. But he who like dumb cattle despises the heavenly, he lives without knowing why, for he merely understands the earthly and only that which is mortal, and sees only as much as is seen by the blind mole. But few, yes all too few, are those to whom God has given the faculty to see what is above them."

Back in the purer air of the Abbey, Tycho compiled all he had observed and made notes about the new star. He had re-

[7] There were notable exceptions to those of whom Tycho complained. Science and an academic training were highly valued by Johan Friis, Herluf Trolle and Peder Oxe in the days of Frederik II, and later by Niels Kaas, Arild Huitfeld and Jacob Ulfeld, and by the greatest of all, Henrik Rantzau.

ceived reports from many German friends as to their views of it. Many, among them Calvin's coadjutor, Theodore Baza, thought it the same star that had shown the Three Wise Men the way to find the Saviour. The Italian Frangipani thought the star the lost Electra of the Pleiades. The German painter Busch wrote: "It was a comet, a poisonous mist, turned to fire by the wrath of God." Tycho had, as recounted, already spoken to Pratensis and Dancey about his thrilling observations; now he wrote his Copenhagen friends that he wished to refute all the nonsense that was being said and written about the star, yet hesitated publishing anything owing to all the censure and sneers it would bring down upon his head.

Pratensis and Dancey and Peder Oxe, the Master of the Court, all wrote back insisting upon Tycho's publishing his theories and telling him to rise above the criticism of ignorant fools. "There is no reason," said Oxe, "why a nobleman should hesitate publishing what he has in mind, particularly if he is disseminating useful information." Pratensis promised to help with the publication.

The three to whom Tycho had appealed in the matter were, with the addition of Vedel, his closest friends and most trusted advisers. Charles Dancey (Carolus Danzæus), the French Ambassador and a Calvinist, had been at the courts of Francis I and Henry II, and also had been a friend of the great constable, Duke Anne de Montmorency. Dancey's position was often difficult, particularly so when he was obliged to give the Lutheran monarch, Frederik II, an account of what had happened in Paris on St. Bartholomew's night. Often his government "forgot" to pay him, and it cost a considerable sum to take part in the lavish ceremonies of coronation and baptism, to say nothing of being godfather to Prince Ulrik. Oxe was the all-powerful, high-minded and upright Master of the Court. Pratensis, the greatest physician of his day, was the learned son of a Frenchman by the name of Philippe de Pré. He was a true son of the Renaissance in his fondness for antiquity and its sciences and for Latin letters and poetry; he belonged to it by his empirical study. Once in writing to him, Tycho stated that there was practically no one else with whom he could discuss the things that really interested him. His early death was a sad blow to Tycho.

Up to now Tycho's only publication had been the Latin effusion about his still-born twin brother. His friends finally overcame his scruples and in 1573 Lorentz Benedict published in Copenhagen *De nova stella,* an octavo of fifty-two pages, consisting of a letter to his friend Pratensis, a section dealing with astronomy and a Latin Elegy to Urania.[8] The publication created a great commotion, not only among Danish scientists, but among scholars throughout Europe, for it was astonishingly correct in every detail relating to the star and, what was more, testified to the work of a mature scholar and a scientist of great sobriety of mind. From now on Tycho's reputation was secure among all whose opinion he valued.

In this, his first book, Tycho said: "Other laudable work awaits me. I have spent enough time on the heavens, my studies and chemistry; and you, my native country, and my friends have taken your share. I must see the world. It now remains for me to travel about the world, on its highways and byways. I want to see what is beautiful in this wide world, what human industry here and there has invented and to learn the customs of all kinds of people. The rush of youth and an inborn craving bids me see much more and learn much about the glorious arts. . . ."

In the first two chapters of the book Tycho took up various matters, rectifying previous theories as to the course of the sun and "his sister, the moon." This was followed by a description of no less than eight hundred fixed stars; he assigned to each one of them its place according to its longitude and latitude at the time of writing. Finally he gave a rectification of the positions of the stars in Cassiopeia's constellation. In the Latin poem

[8] It was later reprinted in his *Astronomiæ instauratæ progymnasmata,* a facsimile of which was printed in 1901.

which concluded the work he deplored the way of living of his social equals, excepting, of course, that of his Uncle Steen.

A contemporary English author, referring to the portions of the book in which Tycho describes "his" star, says: "In divulging much according to the strange and wonderful star, he thought it meet in the former part of the book to treat of some things in general, thereby to lay a groundwork, not only to the explanation of the star, but also to the whole science of astronomy."

Tycho himself stated: "Moreover this star, of which I purpose chiefly to treat, albeit it were ascititious and changeable, yet because it shined forth most miraculously, and contrary to the laws of nature, even in the highest firmament, like to the other natural stars, and stood there fixed and immovable for the space of a whole year and more, it seemed fit that some diligent pains should be taken in considering and unfolding the circumstances belonging thereunto. . . . I have weighed the opinion of those who have either come near unto the truth or wandered from it, concerning this new star. I have written so the truth might appear and shine forth more clearly. . . . This star did at first in his magnitude exceed the whole globe of the earth and was three hundred times bigger than the whole circumference thereof. . . . It shone forth with a jovial, clear and bright luster . . . with a martial, fiery glittering. . . . In the third partition [of the book] I have compared the opinions of other men concerning that matter and examined them by the touchstone of truth."[9]

For several years Tycho had practiced making up at the beginning of each year a sort of almanac for his own use, so he decided to include in the little book the astronomical and meteorological diary that he had prepared for the year 1574, giving the time of the rising and setting of the principal stars, the aspects of the planets and the phases of the moon, together with their probable influence on the weather.

[9] From an early English translation.

De nova stella completed, two further events absorbed his attention at that period—the excitement of an eclipse of the moon and the sadness of burying an illegitimate daughter, Kirstine, who was born in October 1573 and died in September 1576. On her tombstone in the Helsingborg church Tycho placed the inscription: *Filiola naturalis*. In his notebook he recorded: "She died of the plague, two years, eleven months, eleven days and eleven hours old."

The hubbub and excitement of the publication of the book over, Tycho once more began to cast longing eyes on Germany. It was evident in the Elegy that his mind was turning in that direction. He also ordered more instruments made in Copenhagen, astounding the makers by seeming to know more about the art than they did themselves. However, matters arose that temporarily hindered his departure, the first a misfortune, the second a social catastrophe. The misfortune consisted in his suffering from *febris intermittens*, the ague. Cold sensations crept up his back, he was constantly shivering, his teeth chattered, he had a high fever and sweated copiously. Finally his temperature fell and blessed sleep returned. The catastrophe was his marriage: he took unto himself a quiet, domestic girl named Kirstine, who was either a peasant's daughter at Knudstrup or a maid of his uncle's at Herrevad Abbey.

For a nobleman of Tycho's day to take a bondswoman, an "unfree," as his wife, was practically unheard of and entirely scandalous.[10] His relatives, with the exception of his Uncle Steen and his sister Sofie, were infuriated, and the men and women of his own class thought that he had hopelessly disgraced the nobility. King Frederik finally had to intervene to still the outcry. Tycho himself at the time probably gave little thought to the consequences. He wanted a companion and helpmate, by whom he might beget many children, who would look after his house, superintend the servants and kitchen, keep the apprentices in

10 Yet in Sweden, Erik XIV, who became king in 1560, made a love-match with the peasant girl Karin Månsdotter. His nobles attempted to excuse it, asserting it was probably done during one of his frequent fits of insanity.

order and never bother him or be in his way, and who would not be nagging him to take her up to court in Copenhagen or to give her dresses and jewelry. She was to work and not to be seen. Kirstine, he thought, would cause him no trouble. She would, on the contrary, agree smilingly to all he said, purr over his socks and never remonstrate at his eccentricities. Tycho's eldest daughter, Kirstine, *filiola naturalis*, died in 1576, as we have seen, but her mother dutifully bore him several sons and daughters[11] and served him faithfully until the day of his death, which she survived by only three years. Tycho seldom mentioned her in his voluminous correspondence and surely did not prize her as highly as he did his irreplaceable instruments or books. A contemporary speaks of Kirstine as "of an admirable and, to her husband, satisfying fecundity." Says a German biographer, with typical German praise: *Eine tüchtige Hausfrau, und Mutter mehrerer Kinder.*

The marriage laws of those days were somewhat confused. Even Martin Luther's wedded life never received the blessing of the church, for he did not consider a church ceremony necessary to legalize a marriage. That most noblemen kept a mistress, and the king several, was understood and generally condoned. But to marry entirely out of one's class was unthinkable. The legality of marriage and the consequent legitimacy of the children was not defined by Danish law until long after Tycho's rash step. Certain conditions had been considered sufficient for the acceptance of marriage, namely "that the woman for three winters carry the key ring on her belt, openly share her companion's bed and board, bear him children and behave like a faithful, honest wife, dallying with no one else." All these conditions were conscientiously fulfilled by Kirstine. But even Sofie Brahe, Tycho's straightforward and courageous sister, who asserted after his death that Kirstine had been married and that her children were consequently legitimate, was smiled at by all concerned.

[11] See the appendix for a brief account of Tycho Brahe's offspring.

[48]

The great Danish playwright Ludvig Holberg says: "I must admit that this match was quite indecent."[12] Others, in an unkind and unnecessarily offensive manner, refer to Kirstine as "Tycho's harlot." A contemporary author writes: "One may say in his defense, first that it was difficult for a *Philosopho* with a metal nose to acquire a noble young damsel, and secondly, as most of Tycho's thoughts were constantly directed towards the vault of heaven, so that he did not notice *Sublunaria*, or what happened on earth, one might to a certain extent pardon him if he did not in this matter follow the custom and *Bienséance*, and particularly as such a distracted *Philosopho* finds less incommodity in so humble a mate than in choosing a lady of family who would turn up her nose when he spent his money on books and instruments."

An English traveler, Fynes Moryson, tells us that Tycho was said "to live unmarried, but keeping a concubine of whom he had many children, and the reason for his so liuing was thought to be this: because his nose hauing been cut off in a quarrele when he studied in a University in Germany, he knew himselfe thereby disabled to marry any Gentlewoman of his own quality. It was also said that the gentlemen lesse respected him for liuing in that sort, and did not acknowledge his sonnes for Gentlemen."

It is to be noted that in those "good old days" couples often lived together after the betrothal[13] (the *matrimonium inchoatum*), since many of the church leaders accepted the old canonical law, contending that the consent of the two parties made the marriage, which therefore really dated from the betrothal. After 1566 such cohabitation was punished.

The long and short of it was that by marrying as he did, Tycho committed *crimen laesae nobilitatis*, not only against his family but against the entire Danish noble caste.

[12] *Jeg bekiender sandelig at dette Parti var ganske uanstændigt.*
[13] J. Nellemann, "Om Ægteskab, Forlovelse," etc. An article about marriage, betrothal, etc., in *Historisk Tidsskrift*, Ser. v, Vol. i. Copenhagen, 1879.

CHAPTER FOUR

When I consider thy heavens, the work of thy fingers, the moon and the stars, which thou hast ordained.— PSALM 8:3

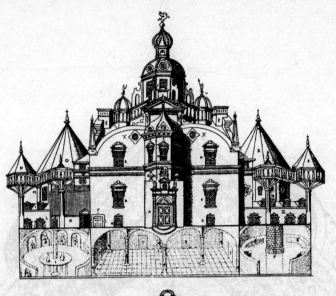

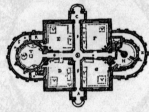

Plan of Uraniborg with Cross Section of Cellars

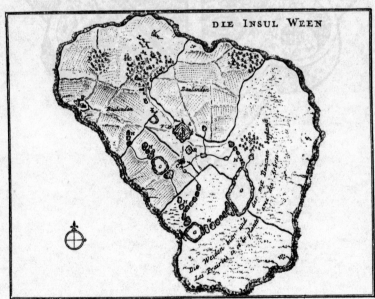

DIE INSUL WEEN

Map of Hveen at Tycho's Time

Uraniborg and Grounds

CHAPTER FOUR

LLNESS and love overcome, with such questionable results, Tycho again began to think of Germany as the place where he might best add to the scientific knowledge of which he already possessed so large a store and at the same time gain some of the general knowledge of the world that he lacked. Then a surprising invitation arrived just as he was jotting down observations of the total eclipse of the moon that had taken place in December 1572. A group of young noblemen, stricken by the temporary craze for scientific knowledge that was now running its superficial course in the capital, had petitioned the king to request Tycho to deliver a series of mathematical lectures at the University of Copenhagen. King Frederik was as amused as he was pleased at this turnabout on the part of some of the young aristocracy, and not only invited Tycho to undertake the work but took particular pains to assure him that it was not below his dignity as a nobleman to lecture. So Tycho came to Copenhagen with his wife in the late summer of 1574 and prepared his work most carefully. Shortly afterwards Kirstine bore him a daughter, Magdalene.

In September 1574 he commenced his course on the Prussian tables, the opening lecture covering in a broad and masterly manner the history and importance of the mathematical sciences.[1] Tycho already offered the opinion that the fate of man did not absolutely depend upon the stars, a skepticism he was to express time and again in his later letters and conversation. With patience, silence and wisdom, he said, one could overcome most difficulties, and one must bear in mind that time changed conditions. As to astronomy: "No society can exist without the subdivision of time into years, months and days, which is the result of astronomical reckoning. Apart from that, astronomy is

---

[1] Tycho's series of lectures was published after his death, in 1610, by a former pupil, Konrad Axelsen (Conradus Aslacus). See bibliography.

[53]

of such a value that a knowledge of it must, for good reason, be desired by every noble and high-minded person. It fills one with tremendous joy and sharpens one's understanding. The knowledge which it imparts raises one's thoughts above the earthly, trivial and passing things to heavenly, elevated and unchangeable considerations."

"Astrology," he said, "did not link the will of man to the stars, for there was something in human beings more elevated than the stars, by virtue of which they could conquer the sinister inclinations of the stars, that is, if they lived truly and in an unworldly manner." Throughout the lectures the boys received a good deal more than they had bargained for, including some entirely new and startling conceptions. Above all they learned what an elusive mistress science is: "Her path, though free and open, is threatened with rocks, storms and breakers."

When free from his university work Tycho would sail across to Scania to visit relatives, see how the paper mill was getting along and visit the chemical laboratory.

In the spring of 1575 the lectures were finished and Tycho at last felt himself free to pack up his instruments and globes. He intended not only to travel to all places in the south where he might learn, meet scholars and purchase books and instruments, but also to seek some congenial spot where he might quietly settle down for good and undertake his lifework. He had little compunction at leaving his family behind, yet in departing begged Pratensis to keep an eye on them until he had decided upon the ideal place to settle.

Tycho went first to visit the Landgrave William IV of Hesse-Cassel, no mean astronomer, of whom he had made a friend through correspondence on mutually interesting astronomical problems. William was not only a real scientist but an able administrator of a well-consolidated little principality. Accounts of his day tell that he was so absorbed a stargazer that when a servant once rushed in to inform him that his castle was afire, he refused to leave his work, merely telling the servant to report the matter to those who might help to put out the blaze. After a week of discussions during daylight hours, and joint observations during the night in the observatory which the landgrave had erected on top of his castle, one of the landgrave's daughters was unfortunately taken so ill that Tycho felt it was embarrassing for his host to entertain him further. He said good-by affectionately, host and guest promising each other to keep up their correspondence and make further visits in a happier future.

Next Tycho went to Frankfort, where his principal object was to pick up treasures for his library at the great book fair, then about to be held. The Fleming, Christopher Plantin,[2] the greatest printer of his day, might well, Tycho hoped, be at the fair. His books were as instructive in their printing, ornamentation, lettering and illustrations as in their contents. Plantin had recently boasted "that he possessed so many stamps, matrixes, presses, characters and figures, that all the printers in Europe asserted they had never seen so many assembled as in his establishment," a statement that had added fuel to the flames of Tycho's desire to discuss printing as well as purchase treasures from him.

Tycho's interest in the printing and binding of books had rapidly developed with the growth of his own library,[3] and he was eager to learn and see everything pertaining to this art that might prove of future service. He browsed among the bookshelves of the *Messe* talking to the learned buyers and sellers, purchasing here and there a copy of particular interest or beauty and taking away with him even more information than volumes.

At Augsburg, his next stopping place, there were of course the old friends, the Hainzel brothers, Johannes Major, Dr. Mylius and the master workmen, to see and to tell all about his life during the last six years. There was one disappointment

---

[2] The Plantin-Moretus printing establishment still stands in Antwerp in its original condition and is one of the chief glories of the city.

[3] Most of his books in existence today are to be found in the Prague University Library.

awaiting him, however, for he was informed that the big quadrant had been damaged by a storm. A pleasanter subject of conversation was *De nova stella*, which was naturally the great topic of many a discussion over numerous glasses at the Ratskeller. Tycho asserted to his eager listeners that the new star portended important changes in state and church, would rob the air of considerable humidity and bring pests and venomous snakes.

The imperial city seemed for many reasons to Tycho an ideal anchoring place and, as Erasmus had said, "the right place for a scholar to settle in." It was one of the most important European centers of learning, well governed by authorities who left one alone. It enjoyed a pleasant climate with generally clear weather, propitious for an astronomer, and harbored many scholarly companions with whom one could study, advise and argue on mutually congenial topics.

There were old friends and he was making new ones, all of whom welcomed him with open arms when he confided to them his plans and ideas. It was the ideal spot. He decided that upon reaching home he would pick up his motley belongings and return with family, instruments and some of his best apprentices. He was now, however, so near to Italy that he determined first to continue south to see Venice and some of the wonders in the northern part of the country, and also to study the classical architecture that Palladio was erecting so successfully.

As usual Tycho absorbed everything avidly during his short Italian visit. He then retraced his steps to Augsburg to see how the construction of his great globe was progressing. While there he persuaded the painter Tobias Gemperlin to steal sufficient time from his portraits to visit Denmark.[4]

Passing through Regensburg (Ratisbon) in 1575, Tycho was present at the coronation of Rudolph II as emperor of the Holy Roman Empire, and to his great satisfaction he made the acquaintance of various men close to the throne, particularly Ru-

[4] It was an unfortunate move for the painter, however, for he died of the plague a few years after reaching Copenhagen.

dolph's chief physician, Thaddæus Hagecius (Hayck). Hagecius and the other new-found friends were later to prove most serviceable to Tycho, so he certainly spent his time profitably before returning to Denmark, carrying with him a manuscript copy of the *Prima narratio* of Copernicus purchased in Regensburg.

When Tycho finally reached home, his mind was made up. He would settle abroad. But before starting to pack, he decided to cross the Sound to take a last look at lovely Scania and to arrange many matters at Knudstrup. Without his knowledge, various friends, including the Landgrave William, who did not wish Tycho to leave, had urged upon King Frederik the tragedy of letting so great an astronomer turn his back on Denmark. The landgrave wrote, "Your Majesty must on no account permit Tycho to leave, for Denmark would lose its greatest ornament whose glory would radiate over his native country." As it happened, the landgrave came to Copenhagen just at this time and took this opportunity to follow up his letter by a personal visit to the king, urging him to take instant steps enabling Tycho to pursue his astronomical studies in his native country. This resulted in the king's sending for Tycho and offering him the choice of several properties. However, none of these seemed to meet Tycho's rather exacting requirements; he left for Knudstrup, grateful to the king but with his plans unchanged.

Fortunately Frederik not only realized the importance of keeping Tycho at home but was genuinely attached to him, as well as being himself interested in scientific pursuits. Deciding to take the bull by the horns, he called a messenger and ordered him to travel night and day until he discovered Tycho and delivered a letter to him. Tycho himself best recounts what happened next, in a letter he wrote to Pratensis,[5] begging him immediately to confer with the dependable Dancey, then to destroy the letter, but to give him as quickly as possible their joint advice in so delicate and difficult a situation.

[5] Wilhelm Nordlind, *Ur Tycho Brahes brevväxling.* Lund, 1926.

"As I," he wrote, "still lay abed early in the morning on February sixteenth [1576], thinking about my German trip and at the same time wondering how I could disappear without attracting the attention of my relatives, and considering all sides of the matter, I was informed, quite unexpectedly, that a royal page had arrived at Knudstrup, who had been waiting during the night to hand me a letter from the king. The page was a nobleman and a relative. The letter instructed me to come at once to the royal hunting lodge at Ibstrup, about a mile from Copenhagen, or wherever the king might be in Sjælland. The king said he had heard from some of his courtiers that my uncle, Steen Bille, had said I intended to go to Germany. He therefore ordered me to come to him so as to get at the bottom of the matter. He stated that he knew I did not want any mark of his favor in the form of a large castle, for I did not want to have the care of it interfere with my studies. When he was recently at Elsinore, where he was building, he had looked out of the window and seen the little island of Hveen, which did not belong to any nobleman. Steen Bille, who was with him, had told him that the island and its location attracted me, so it seemed to the king it might just suit me for both astronomy and chemistry. It had no revenues, but he would take care of that. If I would settle down there he would be glad to give it to me as a gift, and I could live there comfortably without being disturbed. He would sail across as soon as he was through with his building at Elsinore and see how I was getting along, not that he understood much about astronomy, but he would come because he was my king and I was his subject. He asked what I could accomplish abroad that I could not do here at home and said that we should rather see German learned men coming here. He told me to think it all over for a few days and to let him know at Fredriksborg what I thought about it and he wished me to act freely. When I saw him, he would arrange the necessary revenues and the expenses of building, so that I need not worry, but could honor this country, my king and myself."

Pratensis, overjoyed at his friend's good fortune and at the unexpected, happy solution of all his difficulties, immediately wrote to "Noble Tycho" stating that his heart had beaten with joy when he read of the king's offer and that Dancey had been equally glad. Pratensis wrote further that out of gratitude to the king Tycho must abandon all thoughts of going abroad. It was the king's own idea to act as he had, and how could Tycho's relatives now make further difficulties? He concluded by saying Tycho must immediately hurry to the king, who liked to act quickly. This Tycho had the good sense to do.

King Frederik made good his princely offer and Tycho was overjoyed at his good fortune. On February 18, 1576, the king by letter granted Tycho "four hundred good old dalers"[6] until further orders. A few days later the beneficiary inspected the island of Hveen, bringing his instruments with him, and took his first observations there of Mars and the moon. Three months later Frederik issued the following letter:

"We Frederik the Second, etc., make known to all men, that We of our special favor and grace have conferred and granted in fee, and now by this open letter confer and grant in fee, to Our beloved Tyge Brahe, Otto's son, of Knudstrup, Our man and servant, Our land of Hveen, with all Our and the Crown's tenants and servants who live thereon, with all rents and duties which come therefrom, and We and the Crown give it to him to have, enjoy, use and hold, quit and free, without any rent, all the days of his life, and so long as he lives and likes to continue and follow his *studia mathematices*, but he shall keep the tenants who live there under law and right, and injure none of them contrary to the law or by any new impost or other unusual tax, and in all ways be faithful to Us and the Kingdom, and attend to Our welfare in every way and guard against and prevent danger to the Kingdom.

Actum Fredriksborg, the 23rd of May, Anno 1576.
FREDERIK."[7]

[6] A daler at that time was worth about twelve of the present Danish kroner, i.e., about $2.50.
[7] J. L. E. Dreyer, *Tycho Brahe.* . . . Edinburgh, 1890, p. 86-87.

Christofer Valkendorf, the chancellor of the exchequer, had made his early reputation as governor of Bergen, where he had been the first to curb the insolence of the powerful Hanse merchants. He became one of the most remarkable Danes of his day, fulfilling the duties of the king when the monarch was absent and heading the regency during the minority of Christian IV. He was instructed, on the same day as the letter quoted, to pay Tycho four hundred dalers for the expenses of erecting a building on the island of Hveen, for which it was stipulated Tycho himself was to provide certain building materials.

Fortune was indeed smiling upon Tycho Brahe in his thirtieth year. He could not have been treated more handsomely, nor would King Frederik have acted as he did, had he not had the highest regard for Tycho's rare talents and understood what luster they might shed on Denmark.

For the next few months Tycho was extremely busy obtaining labor, purchasing the initial building materials, working on his plans with his architect, digging foundations on the site finally selected and making arrangements for the grand ceremony of laying the cornerstone. The cornerstone of Uraniborg, as his new home was to be called, was finally laid at the southwest corner of the house, level with the ground, on August 8, 1576, by the French Ambassador, Charles Dancey, who had requested the honor and had provided a porphyry block bearing the inscription:

REGNANTE, IN DANIA FREDERICO II, CAROLUS DANZÆUS
AQUITANUS R.G.I.D.L.[8] DOMUI HUIC PHILOSOPHIÆ
IMPRIMISQUE ASTRORUM CONTEMPLATIONI, REGIS DECRETO
A NOBILE VIRO TYCHONE BRAHE DE KNUDSTRUP EXTRUCTAE
VOTIVUM HUNC LAPIDEM MEMORIA FELICIS AMPICII
ERGO P. ANNO CIↃ . IↃ . I, AUGUSTI.

Tycho was in reality quite a Greek in his conception of life. He was a sensitive artist as well as an extraordinary scientist.

[8] *Regis Galliarum in Dania Legatus* [*posuit.*] The envoy to Denmark of the King of the Gauls [placed this stone.]

Everything he touched, whatever he surrounded himself with, must be finished and beautiful, be it a printed page, an instrument, a book binding, or merely a water cock. His artistic sense was developed by his visit to Italy, then in the midst of its classical revival, and also by his contact with the Augsburg craftsmen who produced exquisite Renaissance workmanship in their crowded ateliers.

The ceremony took place amid great festivities. Tycho was surrounded by friends, courtiers and learned men, Vedel of course among them, "at a time when the sun was rising together with Jupiter near Regulus, while the moon in Aquarius was setting." Speech-making, feasting and drinking continued during the greater part of the day, until such guests as were able to leave were placed upon the boats that were there ready to sail back to Sjælland.

The island of Hveen seemed ideal for Tycho's purposes for two reasons: ease of celestial observation and difficulty of access for unwanted visitors. It lay in the middle of the Sound off a point a little more than halfway between Copenhagen and Elsinore, directly opposite the Swedish town of Landskrona. Its white cliffs rose steeply out of the sea, with about two thousand acres of flat tableland, bathed in sunshine or shrouded in fog. The busy water thoroughfare it bisected was even in Tycho's day thronged with the high hulks of men-of-war, scurrying merchantmen and fishing smacks, while around its cliffs whirled the restless, shrieking gulls. The breeze frisked and skipped amid the grass on the edges of the cliffs, before hurrying out over them to ride the waves. The unceasing winds that swept it were, on fair days, full of sunshine, white sails and the slanting wings of birds. Its air was laden with salt and other pungent fragrance, and a divine freshness and brightness hovered over the surrounding stretches of coarse grass. It was ever awake to the surge and tumble of the sea. This island of Hveen, then, was Tycho's world—the chance to build anything he wanted, in any way he wished, with a large and generous purse prepared to defray almost any expense. With the exception of stargazing,

nothing was more congenial to him than building. In considering his problem he turned for advice, as he did very frequently,
to his good and cultivated friend and donor of the cornerstone,
the French envoy, Dancey. His advice was: "Build something
out of the ordinary." Tycho certainly followed the suggestion.
His ideas, in conformity with the age in which he lived and the
society to which he belonged, were grandiose. He fortunately
had an excellent sense of proportion, as well as a true feeling
for beauty that restrained him from producing anything that was
either ridiculous or gaudy.

A time had been reached when protection against attack was
no longer requisite in a nobleman's castle. One could build as
one's fancy dictated. The style most usually adopted in sixteenth
century Denmark was termed "Renaissance," but it differed
radically from every classic feature characterizing this style in
its Italian homeland, with the possible exception of some of its
ornamental detail. It was rather Flemish architecture, brought
to Denmark by the many excellent builders, architects and
craftsmen who had been encouraged to immigrate from the Low
Countries. However, the general plan of Tycho's building and
the distribution of its various rooms had certainly been influenced by what Tycho had seen of Palladian architecture during
his Italian visit. Apart from its ornamentation, the symmetry and
geometrical simplicity of this Italian way of building had evidently appealed to him, for he found himself ready to make use
of its principles in his own construction.

The plan as well as the surroundings of Uraniborg (so named,
of course, after Urania, the muse of astronomy) must surely
have been drawn by Tycho's own compass and ruler.[9] To carry
out his magnificent plans he needed an architect. Since Hveen
was a royal estate merely held in fee for life by Tycho, it was
only natural that the architect selected should be Hans van
Paschen,[10] a Dutchman by birth, high in favor with the king,

---

[9] His talent for architecture was recognized by his brother Knud when he asked
Tycho to assist him in certain work in his castle of Engelholm.

[10] Also referred to as "Passke."

with whom he was constantly conferring while erecting the castle of Kronborg at nearby Elsinore.[11] Some of the more skilled workmen were foreigners who had come to practice their trade in Denmark, while much of the simpler work was done by inhabitants of the island commandeered for the purpose. They hated it, and when Tycho asked his dwarf Jeppe what he would advise to pacify them, he replied, "Give them plenty of strong beer when they grumble." Tycho followed this advice, generally with good results. If it did not succeed, he clapped them in jail.

During the early period of building operations, van Paschen furnished the designs and supervised the construction, sailing over frequently from his work at Elsinore. Tycho himself, according to his agreement with the king, furnished the stone, bricks, cement, timber and other building material. As the work progressed, for some reason or other another architect from the Low Countries, Hans van Stenwinckel of Antwerp, took over, probably when he succeeded van Paschen as royal masterbuilder. They were both able and conscientious, and Tycho retained their friendship in later years, when they frequently came to visit him as guests instead of as advisers. When the workmen were through with their day's work Tycho often gave van Stenwinckel lessons in geometry and astronomy. Wishing to improve an intelligent mind was very characteristic of Tycho.

The building was, and remained as long as it stood, quite unique in Danish architecture, showing strongly the contemporary Dutch influence. Its great fault, from the point of view of design and good taste, was its overelaboration, partially occasioned by the unusual and strange uses for which it was intended. Even King Frederik, overgenerous as he proved to be, probably would not have given architect and astronomer

[11] His salary was "free quarters, 100 daler, a court costume, 1 ox, 2 pigs, 4 lambs, 4 geese, ½ barrel of herring, ½ barrel of butter, 1 barrel of cod, 2 pounds of milk and 4 pounds of malt."

quite as free a hand had he not harbored the thought that Uraniborg might someday become the center of astronomical study and discovery in northern Europe. As it was, when the time came for Tycho's departure, he and the king had probably each spent some 75,000 daler on Hveen's different establishments and its many costly instruments, machinery, books and furnishings.

Uraniborg was not a large building at all, only some 37 feet high, the main square structure having sides only 49 feet long, with semicircular bays on the northern and southern façades, 18 feet in diameter, while smaller two-storied bays in the center, to the east and west, served as entrances. The angles of the square pointed exactly to the four points of the compass.

The exterior was of red brick, with limestone trimmings, elaborately coped and ornamented. Elliptical gables, broken in their centers, terminated the east and west walls, with stone obelisks crowning their angles. The bays were covered with conical copper roofing fitted with openings for stargazing. Around the north and south bays were lesser points of observation mounted on wooden pillars and connected by galleries. The entire structure was crowned by a somewhat absurd two-storied lantern, with a weathervane representing Pegasus. Excellent stonemasons must have been employed to carry out the rich carving—a simple matter, however, in comparison with the work they executed in those days at Kronborg, Frederiksborg, Rosenborg, the Royal Exchange, and the various great castles then being erected by the king and by noblemen in Jutland and the Danish islands.

Tycho's castle stood in a raised circular court, surrounded by flowered parterres, outside of which lay the orchard, the whole enclosed by 18-foot high walls. In the centers of each wall a semicircular bay enclosed an attractive pavilion or arbor. The total span of the four walls was 248 feet. Entrance paths bisected the entire construction from north to south and

east to west. The east-west path led to vaulted entrance gates,
the western one serving as the approach to the castle. Over the
main portal was a dog kennel, from which its inmates could
warn the owner by their barking that an outsider was approach-
ing. Over the eastern portal was a room in which rebellious
tenants might be locked up. The other angles terminated, one,
in a tiny structure serving as a printing establishment, the
other in an apartment used as servants' quarters.

With great skill the designer had linked castle and garden
in a most harmonious manner, each setting the other off. When
in a jovial mood or when the night was warm, the host would
entertain his guests at meals in the little pavilions. The surrounding ashlar-faced walls gave the owner a certain protection and privacy, and had the added advantage of providing
loopholes in case of trouble.

In the high, well-lit cellar were the chemical laboratory
with its sixteen furnaces, a small prison and various storage
rooms, so highly necessary at that age and in that climate. The
laboratory likewise had an oven for glass-making where colored glass was manufactured, not only for Uraniborg's own
use but for highly prized gifts to favored visitors and friends.
On the first floor of the main building were a 125-foot well
and four rooms, all called "guest rooms," rather a strange
provision since privacy had been one of the owner's objects in
coming to the island. One of these rooms was used as a sitting
room in winter, another contained the great mural quadrant,
the most interesting object of all the strange and novel equipment. It consisted of an arc with a 6.75-foot radius, 5 feet
broad and 2 inches thick, furnished with two sliding sights.
The wall on which the quadrant was mounted was adorned
with a painting of Tycho with a dog at his feet, the former
dressed as if expecting cold weather during his work. One hand
points to an aperture in the opposite wall, the other to an open
book on the table at which he is sitting. Back of him was depicted a cross section of Uraniborg, giving an excellent picture

of the contents and decorations of the rooms. The portrait was painted by Tobias Gemperlin,[12] whom Tycho had induced to come to Denmark from Augsburg, and the Uraniborg interior was by the king's Kronborg painter, Hans Knieper of Antwerp.

The circular bay at one end of the building contained Tycho's library and museum, which led to an outside aviary. The students who were not observing or experimenting studied there during the daytime. The second bay housed the kitchen with its well and was connected with one of the adjacent guest rooms, which must have been used as a dining room, likewise connected by a stair with the storeroom below. The second floor had a large summer sitting room, a red, a blue, a green and a yellow room. The first two, also called the "King's" and "Queen's" rooms, were evidently intended to be used as special guest rooms whenever the sovereigns might honor the astronomer by a visit. Both bays served as the main observatories, leading by the aforementioned passages to the smaller instrument towers. In what must have been a most uncomfortable attic, hot in summer and frigid in winter, lodged some eight apprentices, with no heat except what might penetrate from the big stoves in the lower stories. The stoves were built of hard stone (practically impervious to heat) which had been sailed down from Bergen, Norway.

The principal rooms had the truly extraordinary innovation of running water, in this anticipating modern plumbing by several centuries. The excellent water in the cellar well was forced up through lead pipes by a pressure device to a tank, probably located in the cupola, and from there was distributed through pipes hidden in the walls. When a cock was turned, four figures surrounding the cupola commenced revolving and spouting water up in the air as ornamental fountains. The king was so impressed with the accounts of it that he begged Tycho to as-

[12] He painted various portraits of Danish noblemen and entered the service of King Frederik II.

sist in the laying-out of the water system of Kronborg, then about to be installed. All the materials had come from Nuremberg and had been installed by the skillful German plumber, Laubenwolf. It was a great period for practical jokes, and nothing amused Tycho more than secretly to turn the cock, when showing unsuspecting guests this portion of his wonders, and give them a good sprinkling.

While the entire water installation probably originated in Tycho's own mind, such a luxury as running water in one's bedroom was unknown to either Hampton Court or the Louvre in that day! Just how Tycho obtained his water pressure is not known, but it is believed to have been by a pressure pump in his well. It is not easy to understand why his ingenious device for providing the comfort of running water in various parts of the house was not copied and adopted by others.

In the lantern crowning the central building were clock works controlling two exterior dials, and there was also an internal one in the ceiling, giving both the time and the direction of the wind. An octagonal gallery ran around the exterior of the lantern, connecting with two smaller domed structures, surrounded by allegorical figures.

It is a wonder the architect did not lose his mind in trying to solve the many new problems with which the owner confronted him, what with the hitherto unheard-of contraptions Tycho wished arranged and the instruments he ordered installed. No one had ever dreamed of such a building, but as Tycho found a method or device for every one of his impossible demands, the architect executed them. In the working rooms, bare walls surrounded instruments, books, benches, tables and beds, the latter being required because there were often two shifts in the night work, or because Tycho might care to rest between observations. The main rooms were, in contrast, elegantly decorated with carved and beamed ceilings and paneling, some of the walls being covered with gilt and stamped "Spanish" leather. Here and there was prominently painted the motto, *"Non haberi sed esse."* (Not to seem, but to be.)[13]

Uraniborg was located in the very center of the island. Close outside its southeastern angle Tycho erected, four years after Uraniborg had been started, another much smaller building which he called *Stellaburgus* or *Stjerneborg*, "the Castle of the Stars." This was built with exclusively scientific aims in view, and, with the exception of its cupolas, was built under the ground, where the wind could not affect its many instruments and the observations would consequently prove the more reliable.

Stjerneborg, also built by van Stenwinckel, consisted merely of a small central square chamber connected with four circular ones, of which only the two northerly were of equal diameter. The central, heated room, called a *Hypocaustum*, had an alcove where Tycho might nap if the sky was cloudy, and also one for students when not at work.

The circular crypts housed the following instruments: a great equatorial armilla (*Ingens instrumentum armillare*), a revolving quadrant, with a 153-cm. radius, a zodiacal armilla, a great steel quadrant (*Quadrans magnus chalebas*) and a 4-cubit sextant, resting on a revolving globe (*Sextans Trigonicus*). The instruments were all set on stone pillars, easily reached by circular steps. Outside, on Stjerneborg's platform, were set up Ptolemaic rulers as well as movable armillas.

To inspire the assistants, Stjerneborg's walls were ornamented with portraits of great astronomers—Timocharis, Hipparchus, Ptolemy, Albattani (Albategnius), King Alfonso X of Spain, Copernicus and Tycho himself. He was in good company. The entrance of the little building was framed by an Ionic portal with three crowned lions carved in porphyry. Below them Tycho had cut:

NEC FASCES NEC OPES

SOLO ARTIS

SCEPTRA PERENNANT.

[13] On Tycho's memorial in Prague a small tablet bears the inscription *"Esse potius quam haberi."*

Mural Quadrant at Uraniborg

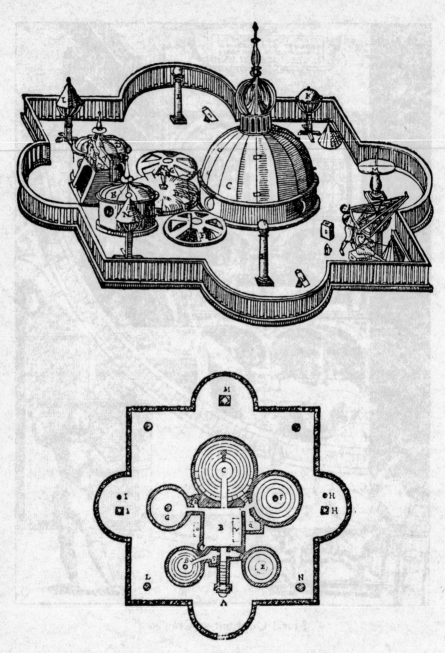

Bird's Eye View of Stjerneborg with Plan

"Neither worldly power, nor riches—art alone survives." The stone may today be seen in the Museum of the Swedish University of Lund.

Tycho mentions his reasons for erecting Stjerneborg, of which he gives the following description: "The towers which were built to the north and south of the main castle of Uraniborg were certainly sufficiently large to contain quite a few instruments, however large such might be: but as I intended for various reasons to procure others, which could not be conveniently placed there without crowding those already installed, I built at a later date, about the year 1584, some seventy paces to the south of the castle, a subterranean observatory with crypts, constructed entirely of masonry. I wished to set up there, firmly and securely, some of the principal instruments, which thus would not be affected by the wind and which likewise could be more easily handled [than in the castle]. I could thus successively and in an orderly manner distribute the students, when there were several of them, so that I might show some in the main castle, and some in these crypts, how to take their observations, without their getting in each other's way or comparing their observations before I permitted them to do so. I called this observatory in Danish, Stjerneborg, which sounds about the same in German, and in Latin is *Stellaburgus*."

"*Insula Venusia, vulgo Hvenna,*" as Tycho at times wrote, when referring to his island, contained some forty farms, most of whose tenants lived in the tiny village of Tuna on its northwestern end, with St. Ib's Church not far away on the very edge of the cliffs, all but tumbling over into the Sound. The land on the island was tilled in common and there were good grazing grounds for the cows and horses at the opposite end of the little island from the village. Then too, there was plenty of good water[14] and a number of smaller and larger ponds, the possibilities of which Tycho's alert mind at once recognized, and there was also game and fish for the Uraniborg table.

---

[14] Still excellent today in its old well.

In addition to Uraniborg and Stjerneborg, Tycho built in their immediate vicinity farm buildings, a house for his instrument-maker, his printing establishment, his own paper mill, a mill for grinding his corn, and places to prepare the hides and parchment for the covers for his finer books. He left nothing undone that his skill could accomplish or ingenuity devise.

Gradually most of the Uraniborg rooms had instruments set up in them as these were finished by Tycho and his apprentices, or arrived from Germany, and particularly from the famous Augsburg makers. Curiously enough, he would never tell questioners how he devised them, wanting the secrets of their wonders to remain his. There were twenty-eight of them in all. In the large northern observatory were a triquetrum of peculiar construction, with an azimuth circle 16 feet in diameter, a sextant of a 4-foot radius for measuring distances and a double arc for measuring smaller distances. In the large southern observatory Tycho set up a vertical semicircle turning around a vertical axis and furnished with a horizontal circle for measuring azimuths and also a triquetrum, a sextant with a 5.5-foot radius for measuring altitudes, and a quadrant of a 2-foot radius with an azimuth circle. In each of the two smaller observing stations was an equatorial armillary sphere.

In the aperture in the south wall of the room containing the great mural quadrant, already mentioned, was a cylinder of gilt brass, projecting at right angles to the wall, on the sides of which the observer sighted with one of the sliding sights. The magnificent 5-foot globe, which had cost 5,000 daler and had taken years to manufacture in Augsburg, was set up in the library when it arrived and was surrounded by Tycho's precious books and pamphlets, tables and portraits of astronomers and philosophers. The globe was a wonderful representation of the celestial sphere, with Tycho's observations engraved on its brass coating. It called forth the admiration of the learned coming from all over Europe to gaze upon it. It bore the following inscription: "In the year 1584 while Frederik II ruled Denmark, Tycho

Brahe, Otto's son, had this globe made for himself and his successors and made it correspond with the arrangements of the heaven." While its construction slowly progressed in Augsburg, Tycho during several visits had given it much of his time, and his powerful friends, the brothers Johannes Baptista and Paul Hainzel, had spent fully as much time around it as around the imperial council table. While it was still in Augsburg, no distinguished visitor came there without being taken to see its progress.

The very last piece of work to be done at Hveen was the laying out of Tycho's flower beds, garden paths and playgrounds, the planting of some three hundred fruit trees, and the stocking of his ponds with fish and his thickets with birds. Here he hoped, when not at work, to listen to the swallows returning and to the croaking of the frogs; and to welcome the mighty Niels Kaas and Jørgen Rosenkrantz or his less famous cronies, Eske Bille, Steen Maltesen Sehested and Niels Krag.

Uraniborg was now ready for its occupants and their astronomical work. Tycho's contemporaries considered the work he had executed grandiose and beautiful. Though they confessed they did not understand it, they felt it was proudly conceived and well worth preserving for future generations.

If today one could suddenly see Uraniborg, the astonished observer would probably exclaim: "Who on earth planned that fantastic, Hans Christian Andersen fairy-tale castle?" But then today is not the sixteenth century, an age when one said and did pretty much as one pleased, that is, if one could afford it. It was a perfectly natural age, and a joyous, exuberant, colorful one, whose grown children expressed in stone as well as in words their ideas of the beautiful or picturesque, just as they sensed them. And Uraniborg Tycho conceived of as something very grand, and thus fitting for his work.

CHAPTER FIVE

*If I beheld the sun when it shined,
or the moon walking in brightness. . . .*
—JOB 31:26

LL these building operations and the purchase or manufacture of the costly and elaborate instruments entailed a lavish expenditure of money. It was thus fortunate, as well as necessary, that King Frederik and the "royal mathematician," as Tycho was now styled, saw much of each other. Tycho was indeed lucky in having a patron whose purse-strings were open and whose purse was filled. Besides, the king was an unusually pleasant fellow, as kings went in those days. Both he and his son, Christian IV, were full of a certain boisterous horseplay and kindly humor belonging to their day. Though court etiquette was strict, the king knew how to banish it when he and his nobles, who surely must at times have included Tycho, sat down for a jovial meal including considerable hard drinking. King Frederik would arise in the midst of it and announce: "Gentlemen, the king is not at home," which was the signal that joy might for the time being be unconfined, and everyone present could do and say pretty much what he pleased. The moment, however, the king again arose and shouted above the din: "Gentlemen, the king has returned," the noisy company would once more be obliged to behave itself.

His able chancellor, Christofer Valkendorf, had an office which was no bed of roses, for the king was constantly pestering him with orders for one thing and another. He might wish warm winter cloth sent his court tailor, "for," writes Frederik, "you know well how cold it is in the great palace halls, and my clothes are thin." He might wish more watchmen engaged for the Copenhagen streets, not only to arrest drunkards and brawlers, but to chase outside the city gates and walls the many pigs roaming about the streets. The king "nearly tripped over one the other night." He might desire that the French shoemaker be ordered to stick to his last and not absent himself so often from his shop. "Best of all, send him to Antvortskov Castle, where he himself could 'look into his seams' "—that is, see what he was about. Again, the chancellor would have to see that Frederik's various cities—and particularly those on the other side of the Sound!—sent him pewter dishes, linen, cloth and candlesticks for his coronation, and he had to obtain the requisite amount of red cloth to make Our Lady's Church gay for the occasion. Or wine, sugar and spices had to be sent to the princes at school, so that Frederik need not be bothered thinking about such things when he was out hunting. Often the sixteenth century language in which the missives were dictated is even quainter and more ridiculous than the official orders themselves.

King Frederik had worried first his father, and then, when he was gone, his councilors, by not marrying until he was thirty-seven. He had, it is true, cast "sheep's eyes" on the pretty daughter of one of his father's councilors, but that romance was nipped in the bud. Having had his fling, he finally resigned himself to the innocuous North German princess, Sophia of Mecklenburg. He found her "a safe, obedient and sensible helpmate," and what more could a king want? He invariably referred to her as "my Sophia."

Frederik was in reality very much of a *pater familias*—of a large family, and one in whose smallest concerns he took the liveliest interest. We read that he fussed about the pheasants that a Dutch woman had not delivered as promised. To the kitchen he complained that the castle gatekeeper admitted too many of the city women into his courtyard to draw water at its well, who then, instead of going about their business, remained there to gossip. He fussed about casks of Rhenish wine and barrels of Rostock beer not arriving for the big party he was planning. After the party he complained of a headache and noticed spots on his breeches and so ordered new cloth from England and foxskins from the Duchies for new suits. Again, he pondered over what except drink might keep the city watchman warm on cold nights and what would be the cost of the bell he proposed to present to Our Lady's Church. And even more important, he commanded stone girders and copper for the building he was undertaking at Frederiksborg and Kronborg, for all such palaces as well as the fortresses of his two kingdoms were his personal property as much as his Sophia or his riding boots.

At times the wedding of one or another of his noblemen was held in the king's own palace. To one of these wedding parties we know he invited Tycho and Manderup Parsbjerg who had cut off Tycho's nose, hoping the convivial occasion might patch up matters. But there is no record as to whether a reconciliation was effected on that occasion.

Like most monarchs of his day, Frederik was generally out of cash, but he could and did constantly travel around his domains, he and his retinue being put up by whatever nobleman had the ill-fortune to be living along the king's route. His "progress" meant not only administering justice, but plenty of excellent hunting and hard drinking. For meals for him and his retinue the following was required: one and a half oxen, eight sheep, thirty hens, half a barrel of salt pork, 300 flounders, half a barrel of salt herring, a big cask of butter, and forty kegs of beer; not to speak of the requisite hay and oats for the 280 horses.

Foreigners of distinction who happened to be in the country were generally asked to join in the fun. Thus a gentleman by the name of Von Tenfelt wrote after his return home: "When I was in Denmark with Archduke Matthias, I did not know how to drink until I was taught it and taught it thoroughly by King Frederik. In my present joy at having acquired such knowledge I must say I feel it well worth while to die for such a King, yes, for everyone who comes from Denmark, even be it a Danish dog."

On June 2, 1577, King Frederik was in fine fettle, for after the disappointing appearance of two princesses, Sophia had at last given birth to Prince Christian. So Frederik decided to celebrate the occasion in proper style and invite his cronies, courtiers and a number of his friends to a fitting christening party at the palace. This was a strange mixture of the showy magnificence and the squalor of the times. The state rooms and royal apartments were finished in Spanish gilt leather, inlaid woods and parquetry, marble tiles and crystal chandeliers, with gold and silver services in the cabinets along the walls, while the servants and guards lived in unlit and unventilated holes and niches and dark and crooked passages both above and under the ground, and kitchens, sculleries and serving-rooms were seldom if ever cleaned. The successive buildings of the palace surrounded a closed courtyard around which lay everything required to supply His Majesty's table and convenience, a chapel, an herb and vegetable garden, brewery, laundry, slaughterhouse, stables and kennels, a tailor shop in which were cut and sewed all the clothes of the members of the royal household, wine cellars, cold storage rooms and an armory.

Frederik started the day by ordering all the church bells to be rung, bands to play from the church spires, all the cannon on the ramparts and men-of-war to be fired, and a procession of the citizens to march through the city streets, followed by dancing in the public squares. Among other entertainment for his guests, the king instructed the university authorities to have the students perform a play in the courtyard. After considerable discussion a comedy representing David's fight with Goliath was selected. This proceeded smoothly until the actors reached the place where the Philistines were to flee before the Israelites. Resenting having to take the part of cowards before the king and his court, the actors impersonating the Philistines, instead of fleeing, put up a stout resistance, ending in a real fight between the two armies. Amid the general hubbub the near-sighted old Admiral Peder Skram, who had been given a front-row seat, and whose fighting blood was up, scrambled onto the stage to aid God's chosen people. Others followed him and plunged into the fight on one side or the other. Fortunately the Israelites, more numerously aided by the audience, finally routed the Philistines to the eminent satisfaction of the king.

Tycho was there in the thick of it all and during a quieter moment of the evening was instructed by the king to prepare the newborn prince's horoscope as soon as he returned to Hveen.[1] He

---

[1] When the great Gustavus Adolphus was born in 1594, his father asked Tycho to cast his horoscope. Tycho complied, and in it stated that Gustavus would one day become King of Sweden. His father, Duke Charles, belonged to a collateral

was none too fond of casting horoscopes, and had, in fact, when asked for one by Duke Ulrich of Mecklenburg-Güstrow, father of Queen Sophia, politely replied that he did not really care to busy himself with astrology, but wished to confine himself to astronomy and the marvelous course of the stars. Naturally, however, King Frederik's wishes had to be respected, particularly as Tycho was well aware of the fact that he and the Holstein nobleman Ditlev Reventlov were considered the most famous of all astrologers of their day.

It took him a few weeks (the appearance of a comet intervened, observations and notes on which had to be recorded), but on July 1 Tycho called at the Copenhagen palace with the *"Horoscopus Sr. Regis Christiani IV-ti, ad Mandatum Sr. Regis Friederici II-di."*

The horoscope he delivered to King Frederik is still in its beautiful green velvet binding in the Royal Library in Copenhagen. It starts by giving in drawing and description the position of stars and planets at the birth of the prince. The calculations are in Latin, but the conclusions to be drawn from them, in German. Tycho predicted:[2] "That the Prince's years of infancy are to pass without danger, as Venus was favorably placed in the ninth hour, and though in the second year the opposition of Mercury to the ascending point indicates some small illness, it will be nothing serious. In the twelfth year some serious illness will take place, arising from black bile. In the twenty-ninth year he will have to be very careful both as to his health and his dignity. A very critical time will arise around his fifty-sixth year, when the sun and Mars will be most unfavorable and even Venus cannot help, as she will be in the eighth hour. If he successfully passes that period he will have a happy old age.

"Venus will make him pleasant, courtly and valorous, fond of the arts. Mars will make him bellicose, while Mercury will add adroitness and skill to his other faculties. He will be of a

branch of the Swedish royal family. Not only royal personages, but all who could possibly afford it had their children's horoscopes cast. It was an expensive affair, as the greater and more reliable the astrologer, the greater the cost.
[2] J. L. E. Dreyer, *Tycho Brahe . . .* , p. 140.

sanguine temperament. As Venus and Mars were joined [at his birth] the Prince will indulge too much in sensual enjoyment. He will be healthy and not subject to illness, he will be fortunate in his undertakings and receive many honors and riches. The prospects as to marriage are not too favorable, for he will be more inclined to amours than to matrimony.[3] He will not have many children, as Saturn, the master of the fifth house, is in a sterile sign. Venus shows he will cause his own death by immoderate sensuality!"

When at a later date Tycho was called upon to cast the horoscope of the next son, Duke[4] Ulrik, he stated "that he was to subjugate a widow and marry twice, once a martial and once a jovial wife." In both he proved right. He also performed the same service for the third son, Duke Hans. The horoscope is likewise in the Royal Library at Copenhagen, exquisitely bound in green velvet. It foretold that Hans would die at the age of eighteen, which he obligingly did.

Though Tycho kept a book entitled *Themata genethliaca* in which he entered the horoscopes he had worked out, he did not, as a matter of fact, take much interest in, nor attach much importance to them, for both he and King Frederik believed they were of doubtful value. Astronomy, with the knowledge of the position of the stars, was the true science. Time and again both friends and important and influential personages asked to have their horoscopes cast, but Tycho almost invariably excused himself. In one letter we find him stating that he "did not care to mix in astrological matters and for some years had endeavored to put astronomy in its proper place." This must have been known to friends, for one of them refers to the matter by writing: ". . . and as for astrology which *you* do not care much about. . . ."

As Tycho advanced in wisdom he sifted the false from the true. He did, however, very much enjoy preparing His Majesty's yearly almanac, which was one of his January duties. Like

---

[3] In this Tycho hit the nail on the head, but was scarcely accurate in his next prediction, for, in addition to his legitimate children, Christian produced eighteen illegitimate ones by various mistresses.

[4] Danish princes not direct heirs to the throne bore the title of "Duke."

our well-known "Farmer's Almanac," it contained many interesting facts and much useful advice on what to do in the coming
year, with only minor and pardonable nonsense intermingled.
The king was always anxious to receive it. We find him writing
to Tycho: "Take knowledge of the fact that we wish you would
provide somewhat earlier than usual the almanac which you
have promised us for the year '88. We command and desire you,
in case it is now ready, to give it to the boy who brings you this
letter. Or in case they [?] are not yet ready, please finish them
as soon as possible and let us know when we may expect them.
Do this to please us. Leaving you in the hands of God this 24th
day of September, year 1587."

Another of the duties of the royal mathematician was to keep
the king's instruments in order. Thus Frederik writes him one
day: ". . . We cannot help remembering that we sent you some
time ago a compass which you yourself had made for us, which
had become somewhat inaccurate and that you were to mend it.
If it is now corrected, then we bid you send it to us without de-
lay. If you have not received it then we bid you and desire you
make for us two compasses like the other one and as well and as
quickly as possible, in order that we receive it immediately. Sorø,
December 11, year 1584." At other times it might be an inscription wanted by the king for a clock dial, or advice on something
or other out of order in and about the palace.

While still busied with his building operations Tycho had the
pleasure of realizing that he had become a prophet in his own
country. To his genuine surprise he was offered, on the recom-
mendation of his friend and former teacher, Niels Hemmingsen,
the rectorship of Copenhagen University. It was unusual that
one who was not a "university man," and possessed neither a
doctor's cape nor a professor's title, should be offered such an
honorable and responsible post. But the offer pleased Tycho, as
coming from intellectual equals, and was the type of esteem and
recognition he coveted. It was, however, out of the question for
him to leave Hveen and the study of the heavens—lecturing or
ruling a faculty was not his business. So he thanked them for the

honor but declined, adding that he was always at the service of
the University whenever he might be able to assist it.

This was the heyday of Tycho's good fortune, with King
Frederik's purse open—a perfect horn of plenty into which he
might reach his hand time and again as he hurried over and back
across the Sound to Copenhagen. In addition to building funds
there were also other benefactions. The royal gift might be nothing more than a big brass bell with which to call the household
and laborers to work (yet such things were costly enough in
those days) or a boat in which to cross the Sound, or again some
large and costly favor, such as the manor of *Kullagaarden* in
Scania, with its eleven farms and two manor houses and its new
lighthouse on the promontory of *Kullen*, facing the Kattegat.

This latter gift entailed the responsibility of keeping the light
lit to prevent the fishermen in those waters from going on the
rocks. To this obligation Tycho unfortunately paid no attention,
so an admonitory letter was soon dispatched by the king saying:
"I will not hide from you that I often and constantly receive
complaints from the seafarers in the Sound that the lantern is
without light, and I am more than surprised as I remember that
you have particularly informed me that you had found a better
place for the lighthouse where its lantern could show the seamen
their way."

His Majesty had every reason to remember, for Tycho had
been granted four hundred daler annually from the Elsinore
tolls and customs, for the sole purpose of keeping the light going
winter and summer. Tycho's thoughts being on the stars and
Uraniborg, despite all this generosity and these specific stipula-
tions, still the light often remained unlit and the fishing smacks
went on the rocks. It ended in Tycho's coming within an ace of
losing the property and the governor of Helsingborg taking it
over. Tycho only retained it in the nick of time, by promising to
transgress no more in so slight yet necessary a matter.

Two more pieces of good fortune came his way, the first in the
form of the fief of the Crown estates on Nordfjord, on the northwestern coast of Norway. All their taxes and royal revenues

were in the future to be paid in to the Lord of Knudstrup and Hveen, at least until such time as the income from the canonry of the Holy Three Kings' Chapel of Roskilde fell to him. The Danish cathedral chapters had not been abolished by the Reformation, and their incomes were now being given by the king to men of merit. Their members were still called "prebendaries" or "canons," and the canonries were sinecures which the king assumed the right to bestow. The canonry of the Holy Three Kings' Chapel of Roskilde was thus promised to Tycho on the death of the old canon, Henrik Holk. When Holk obligingly passed away, King Frederik made good his promise and conferred the canonry upon Tycho. All its temporalities were granted him "during pleasure," including the canon's nice little home, its farms and other property, on the condition, however, that proper provision be made "for the daily singing of hymns in the chapel, to the glory of God, sung above the royal tombs by two poor school boys, who were likewise to be kept in clothing and food, so that they would assist the vicars-choral in the daily services." Furthermore, the canonry was to maintain two poor students in the University of Copenhagen and see that both school boys and students were diligent and fitted to devote themselves to learned pursuits. The widow Holk was to be left in peace for a year and to receive a certain revenue with which to keep body and soul together, the laborers on the fief belonging to the canonry were to be treated justly, done no bodily harm and not to be burdened with any new taxes, and finally, the Chapel of the Holy Three Kings was to be kept in good repair as also the royal tombs it contained.

According to Tycho himself, the total income of the prebend amounted to a very considerable, in fact quite a princely, sum for a man of science. How he carried out his obligations in the matter we shall see in due time. The king was even so generous as to allow him to retain the Nordfjord fief with its revenues after the Roskilde revenues had become his. Tycho thus ate his cake and saved it too.

All the main work on Uraniborg was now completed. On November 4, 1580, he wrote to Dr. Thaddæus Hagecius, Emperor Rudolph's physician, that his castle was finished, meaning the principal construction, for a year later he wrote again: "Now at last Uraniborg is completed," indicating that instruments and furnishings were also in place.

Tycho's restless energy and impatience had driven his workmen so hard that they finally rebelled and succeeded in lodging their complaints in such high quarters that Arild Ugerup, the governor of Helsingborg, and Axel Gyldenstierne, the governor of Landskrona, were dispatched by the king to Hveen. Their visit resulted in royal orders clearly defining the future relationship between Tycho and his tenants and the labor he might exact from them.

All that remained to be done at Hveen was to fit and install the last of the interior cabinetwork and the painting and decorations. The great globe had arrived[5] from Augsburg after many impatient letters from Tycho, and Johannes Major had written that he was now prepared to make another one of any size required. In addition to this prize a quadrant had likewise been brought across the Sound on a quiet day.

In his mechanical workshop Tycho's artists and artisans executed the most delicate work in beautiful forms. Both they and his printers and paper workmen were treated with far more consideration than his Hveen laborers and tenants, probably because they were harder to replace. They not only executed astronomical instruments but timepieces and wind instruments; they designed and cast or cut the ornaments of bronze and lead and stone on the building and in the garden. Tycho had, in fact, an atelier of skilled craftsmen, delighting in what they produced, satisfying Tycho's artistic sense fully as much as his mechanical one. The illustrations of the instruments that have come down to us show their astonishing artistic beauty. Those he gradually installed were on a scale and of a type unknown since the days of the great Arab astronomers. He substituted equatorial for zodiacal armillæ, thus definitely establishing the system of measure-

[5] After twenty years of labor the positions of a thousand stars were finally marked on the globe.

ments in right ascension and declination, and improved the grad-
uation of circular arcs by adopting the method of "transversals."
By these means, employed with consummate skill, he obtained
an unprecedented degree of accuracy, and as an incidental though
valuable result, demonstrated the erroneousness of the supposed trepidation of the equinoxes.

Up to the end of the eighteenth century the mural quadrant
was the most important instrument in astronomical observations.
While Tycho took great pride in his, the sextant was his favorite
instrument, and he placed one in the great northern observatory
as well as one in Stjerneborg.[6]

How small a role Tycho's family played in his life is best illustrated by the fact that he very rarely refers to them in his
correspondence. The later, disastrous episode of his eldest
daughter Magdalene's unfortunate betrothal was an exception.
He seldom mentions the small family details that, after all, cannot help playing a certain part in the life of a married man with
numerous children, however great and inattentive a genius he
may be. But life for Tycho was decidedly not a family affair.

Tycho had some ten pupils at a time at Uraniborg. His relationship with them was a domineering one. Teachers were not
to be questioned but to be obeyed. He was their master rather
than their instructor, and as a result most of his assistants were
not drawn to him by the bond of sharing common discoveries and
progress. They were aware of his genius, but could not fully
grasp it. He did not give himself the time to explain, to tell them
the whys and wherefores, except when it was necessary for the
prosecution of their work. They came to him to get on in life
and because of their interest in the science of astronomy itself or
the branches of learning that were considered to relate to it.
Tycho's genius generally inspired them with awe and wonder
rather than with sympathy or affection. Even with the best of his
co-workers, he was constantly at sixes and sevens. No feeling

[6] Copernicus, who tested his new system a century before the invention of the
telescope, had as his primitive instruments a sun dial, a triquetrum, three wooden
rods to measure the altitude of a celestial body, and an astrolabe, a sphere within
vertical and horizontal rings.

[85]

deeper than professional admiration sprang up between him and any of them. It was only the learned, the proficient scientists who enlisted Tycho's heart as well as his head.

The two daily meals were taken together in the dining room, with Tycho at the head of the family board—dinner between nine and ten, or some five hours after arising, and supper at six. Incredible quantities of food were devoured. Such was the custom of the age, possibly fostered by the raw, damp climate of Denmark. Bread and spiced herring washed down with beer was swallowed by each one in his bedroom after rising, added to which a certain number of pots of beer per day were allowed each pupil; these he might drink whenever he pleased. No one was the worse for such a regimen; on the contrary, the lads seemed to thrive on it. The general diet was fish. Everything consumed was highly spiced. Sugar was much prized and, as a substitute, honey. When there were guests there were often either fresh southern fruits, such as sweet or "sour" oranges,[7] and wines imported by the Dutch immigrants, or well-peppered corn brandy. Such occasions were preceded by busy hours in the kitchen where Kirstine was assisted by the milkmaids. Kirstine would supervise and give orders and worry about the proper "presentation" of the dishes of food on the huge silver platters and see that the butter and cheese came out to her satisfaction.

Tycho's apprentices and assistants came from all over Europe, and numbered among them quite a few who later rose to prominence and distinction in astronomy, mathematics, chemistry, theology and medicine. One of them was even permitted by the university faculty to receive the *Stipendium Regium* while studying with Tycho, though this particular scholarship was intended for study abroad. Some became professors, others clergymen and doctors, and four of them became bishops. Many came to Hveen of their own accord, humbly begging to be allowed to work under the great master. Some stayed for years, others only for a few months. In many of them Tycho awoke an enthusiasm

---

[7] "Sour oranges" was the name for lemons.

for their subjects that continued down through successive generations.

The following is a partial list of his pupils:[8]

Peder Jacobsen Flemløs, later a Canon of Roskilde, assistant to Governor Gyldenkrone of Akershus, and editor of the meteorological diary kept at Uraniborg, in which King Frederik was much interested. (See Bibliography)

Gellius Sascerides, Magdalene's faithless suitor

Andreas Wiburgensis [from Viborg in Jutland]

Jacobus Hegelius

Severinus N. (opposite whose name is placed the unflattering description: *turbator, phantasta*)

Elias Olai Cimber (Morsing), one of Tycho's favorites, who stayed at Uraniborg from 1583 to 1597

Joannes Buck Cimber (Colling) = Kolding in Jutland

Andreas Jacobi Lemwicensis [from Lemvig in Jutland]

Otto Wislandus Islandus [from Iceland]

David Joannes Sascerides, brother of Gellius

Jacobus N. Malmogiensis [from Malmö in Scania]

Christiernus Joannes Ripensis [from Ribe in Jutland]

Petrus Richterus Haderslebiensis [from Haderslev in South Jutland]

Johan Isaacsen Pontanus, one of Tycho's best pupils

Juarus Hemmetensis Cimber

M. Nicholaus Collingensis

Martin Ingelli Coronensis

Joannes Hamon Dekent

Christiernus N. de Ebenthood

The names of the three last students indicate their foreign origin. The list was probably kept by Hans Coll (sometimes given as Crol) whose Latin name was Joannes Aurifaber. He was a goldsmith and instrument maker in charge of Tycho's workshop.

Many other pupils besides those mentioned above came and went. An important one was K. Sørensen Longomontanus, later

---

[8] J. L. E. Dreyer, *Tycho Brahe* . . . . Edinburgh, 1890. The list Dreyer gives is quoted from *Danske Magazin*, Copenhagen, Ser. IV, Vol. 2, p. 32.

professor of mathematics at the University of Copenhagen. He built the observatory on the Round Tower, and in 1644 reprinted Flemløs's book on forecasting weather. Then there were Franz Ganzneb Tengnagel who married Tycho's daughter Elisabet in Prague shortly before Tycho's death; and Conradus Aslacus (Konrad Axelsen) from Bergen in Norway who in 1610 published Tycho's lectures on mathematics given at the University of Copenhagen 1574-1575. Other names were, Georg Ludwig Frobenius, Melchior Joestelius, Ambrosius Rhodius, Marius Jacobsen and Paul Wittich from Breslau.

It was no easy matter to be accepted as a pupil. Only students giving promise of real talent were admitted. Thus Tycho writes to one of his friends: "If Victorinus Schönfeld wishes to send his son here to visit me, he may do so, but whenever he or I think the time has come for him to leave, we must both be free to bring this about. It is immaterial to me whether he has or has not become a master of arts. I would rather that he really was one, instead of merely having the degree, but that is no easy matter. It is sufficient, however, that he be a student of science."

When time and the stars permitted, Tycho often quoted the Bible for the edification of the young pupils surrounding him. Said he: "In the first chapter of the Genesis (Book of Moses) it is written that the stars were created not only to tell the years and the month and day but also to be signs unto us," and "In Jeremiah you are told that you need in no way fear the signs of the heavens. In the tenth chapter of the same wise prophet you again read: 'Do not fear the signs of the heavens as do the heathen.'"

In addition to the pupils at Uraniborg, there was, of course, the staff of artists and artisans, generally numbering some twenty in all. Kirstine was responsible for their board and lodging.

Among his able assistants must also be mentioned Tycho's sister Sofie (1556-1643). She was one of the most extraordinary women of her age, high-minded, warm-hearted and learned. She spoke and wrote Latin fluently, knew astronomy sufficiently well not only to assist Tycho, who trusted her absolutely, but actually to participate in his work. She busied herself much with genealogy and had a particular bent for casting horoscopes, so when she traveled she always took her "nativity book" along. She also had a passion for alchemy and chemistry and invented a "pest-elixir" that was sometimes prescribed when the dreaded plague arrived. Alchemy was to be her bane, however, for in her endless experimentation to discover the formula for producing gold, she lost all of her possessions. But if she did not succeed in producing gold, she manufactured many a pill, tincture and powder that friends insisted did them no end of good. Such verses as she left behind her indicate a real poetic gift. In referring to her, Tycho once said: "In themselves women possess great gifts, which are due to the influence of the moon and Mercury which likewise causes most of them to become excessively talkative." Brother and sister often wrote to each other in a jocose vein, Tycho calling her Urania and himself Apollo. Through all of Tycho's misfortunes, early and late, Sofie stood stoutly by him and defended him, even in opposition to the rest of the family.

She was first happily married to Otte Thott *til* Eriksholm in Scania by whom she had a son, Tage, who had a most distinguished career as a statesman. After her husband's death, she was a constant guest and worker at Uraniborg where she met, fell head over heels in love with, and in 1590 became engaged to Erik Lange. Lange's unfortunate passion was likewise alchemy and the search for gold, in which he, in turn, so completely ruined himself that he was forced to flee abroad in order to escape his debtors. Desperate and penniless, yet faithful, Sofie after twelve years of engagement found her lover again in Slesvig. They married in 1602 and both returned to live the last years of their lives quietly with her distinguished son at the family estate of Eriksholm.

In those days the fashion among scholars of Latinizing their names was aped by the apprentices and pupils. Many Scandinavian names thus altered remain in their Latin form today as the family name. On all his publications Tycho printed *"Tychoni*

Brahe Dani . . . ," and at times he signed himself magnificently "*Dominus de Knudstrup et arcis Uraniburgi in Insula Dania Venusia fundator,*" though more generally, "Tygo Brahe." He was Brahe *til* ("to") Knudstrup, not "of," as noblemen signed their names in France, England, or Germany.

Tycho was no easy taskmaster, but exacting and impatient; every detail was of the utmost importance to him and, he felt, should also be so to the pupils. Tycho demanded the same accuracy from every one of them that he himself gave his work. Several of them would often receive orders to give the exact time of simultaneous celestial observations from their different observation posts in Uraniborg, which when they were submitted to him, he could check and cross-check. When the night was past Tycho would go over with each one what he had written down, and compare the notations with his own data. What seemed undoubtedly correct would be entered in a ledger for future classification and printing.

Some of the pupils fell by the wayside, others became infected with their master's lust for labor and intoxication with the work, and a few of them remained lifelong friends, correspondents and assistants from their scattered posts of usefulness and learning.

Though Tycho demanded much of his pupils, yet he himself was the most indefatigable worker of them all. His industry astounded his contemporaries and above all his social equals. Though there is nothing in his own or contemporary biography indicating he ever slept in the daytime, he must have stolen some sleep then, for he frequently spent the night watching the stars. Even when he went abroad it was not for recreation but in connection with scientific matters—all his waking hours were spent discussing them. His industry and application really knew no bounds.

The strangest member of the little Uraniborg community was Jeppe the dwarf, in cap and bells. He was scarcely three feet high, a misshapen, half-witted monstrosity, credited, amid his senseless chatter and babbling, with foretelling coming events.

Strange tales circulated about him and few of the Hveen laborers
and farmers felt wholly comfortable when he was skipping and
rolling about nearby. At mealtimes he would sit like a dog at his
master's feet under the table, and every once in awhile Tycho
would pat his huge head and throw him a morsel, noting such
sayings of Jeppe's as seemed to him important. The assistant
Longomontanus tells us that whenever anyone was ill Jeppe
would prophesy whether he was going to die or not. When
Tycho was absent from the island and the pupils were romping
about, Jeppe would warn of his approach by shrieking, "Junker
paa Landet!"[9]—"The Squire is on land!" [has landed.] Those
nearest to Tycho always called him "Junker Tyge."

As soon as Tycho finally settled down to his methodical astronomical work of observation he gradually began to consider the
possibility of writing and editing a large work, a *Theatrum astronomicum*, covering his whole new theory of astronomy. This
would entail much difficulty, for he felt that the Copenhagen
printers, however capable they had at last become, could scarcely
execute the work in a satisfactory manner. And then, too, he
would constantly be obliged to go to Copenhagen and, with the
suspicion of his age, he feared that anyone sneaking about attempting to discover and steal his inventions would probably succeed in so doing while he was absent. If, on the other hand, he had
a printing establishment of his own, he could safeguard and
publish what he wished. It would be an expensive undertaking,
requiring considerable additional work and the purchase of
German presses and paper and the employment of foreign ex-
perts. But just at present there was so much else that demanded
his immediate attention that Tycho finally decided to let this
matter await a better, freer moment. In addition to the satisfaction of printing his own work, he fully realized the immense aid
the constantly developing art of printing was giving to science.
Up to the present his only publications had been that on the new
star, in which the good Pratensis had proved such a powerful
support; and the subsequent memorial poem to him.

[9] Gassendi, *Tychonis Brahei Vita*. Paris, 1654. (Accounts of Jeppe are based
on reports by the Danish physician Ole Worm.)

"It was not unusual," says his Danish biographer, F. R. Friis, "for learned men of the age to have their own printing establishments, nor was this singularly extravagant, as a printing establishment of the time needed only the simplest tools and arrangement. Tycho had several reasons for doing his own printing. He was constantly writing things that were to be printed, and much of what he wrote could not be satisfactorily printed in Copenhagen, particularly as his writings were full of figures and tables. And then it was important for him to see that nothing of what he printed reached the public before he himself wished it."

One of Tycho's immediate concerns was to procure for his library some much-needed books of reference and every new work that had been published relating to astronomy or the sister sciences. He already possessed a collection of books unusual even for a learned man of his day, including works by Archimedes, Aristotle, Copernicus, Ptolemy, Apollonius and Xenophon, and in the good Knudstrup library he had acquired considerable acquaintance with classical literature. But that did not satisfy him. He wrote to acquaintances all over Europe, among others, to Hugo Blotius, the Emperor's librarian in Vienna, begging him to send whatever was best in mathematics, astronomy, medicine, philosophy or chemistry. The chances were that they would be in Latin, the language of scholars in those days, but it did not matter what language they were written in—Tycho would always be able to puzzle them out. He wrote Vedel to buy all books to be found in Germany dealing with the 1579 comet. He wrote Johannes Major "for goodness' sake to scour the market" with the happy result that back came Scaliger's *De emendatione temporum*,[10] containing the Gregorian calendar reform. He sent his pupils Elias Olsen Morsing (Cimber) and Peder Jacobsen Flemløs to Germany to hunt books. He turned not only to the yearly book fairs and publishers and scientists, but to princes who had their own agents here and there on the lookout for new publications, and to clergymen who seemed to have a particularly "good scent" for them. Many of them browsed about, spending

[10] Joseph Justus Scaliger, Professor at Leyden 1540-1609. See Bibliography.

more time in the bookstalls of their various cities than in their pulpits. Nothing was more acceptable, from friendly visitors, such as Paulus Urtichius (Paul Wittich) of Breslau, than their arrival with a book or two, and in turn, later on, nothing gave Tycho greater pleasure than to send his own publications to such as he believed would value them because of their content as well as their donor. In the end his library numbered some five hundred volumes, comprising all that was of importance in his work published up to his time—quite a sizable collection, though modest as compared with Rantzau's more than six thousand, or the ninety thousand which the emperor's librarian, Blotius, wrote he had on his shelves in Vienna.

During the early building years and the first succeeding ones, the daily routine of Uraniborg was constantly broken by visits of the curious, the arrival of a new apprentice, a royal messenger with money or the landing of crates with German instruments or books. And there were pleasant visits from brother scientists, such as Bongarcius (the Frenchman Jacques Bongars) and Erik Lange, from the cultivated Bishop of Oslo and Hamar, Jens Nilsson, from the Bishop of Bergen, Anders Foss, and the great chancellor, Niels Kaas, whose visit was recorded in Latin verse, as was the death of Tycho's good friend, Hans Frandsen from Ribe.[11]

While the geometrical representation of the planetary system did not satisfy Tycho, he wanted, above all else, to know how the universe was actually constructed. About the year 1582 he rejected all previous systems, including the Copernican, and evolved his own, this being a mixture of the old and the new. Scarcely a day passed without Tycho's pondering over the great question. He asked himself, where did all his labor lead, without clarity and order in the interrelation of the planets? There *must* be some harmony that his observations would never prove unless he could reach out to the truth, the great, underlying principle.

With the wonder and ignorance of thirteen, when he first read Ptolemy's solution, he had accepted without question the epi-

[11] See Bibliography.

cyclic system of the universe, which made the sun and planets move in circles whose centers were themselves in motion upon other circles, the earth being considered at rest. As Tycho grew in knowledge and wisdom, however, this did not satisfy him, and he turned to the Copernican system[12] in the hope that it might solve his knottiest problem. He naturally recognized the sublime qualities of his great predecessor who had died only three years before he himself was born, but unfortunately he could not agree to the fact that the sun was the center of the universe with all other heavenly bodies revolving in concentric circles about it. That Mercury, Venus, Mars, Jupiter and Saturn did so, yes, but the sun and moon must revolve about the earth. He felt so strongly that Copernicus erred, and, later on, that so did his great pupil, Kepler, who leaned towards the Copernican system, that on his deathbed Tycho earnestly begged Kepler to develop a theory of the universe based on his own, the Tychonic, rather than the Copernican system.

According to the latter system, the observation of the complete cycle of Venus had proved that this planet revolved around the sun. But there were also those who said that if the moon revolved around the earth while the earth revolved around the sun, the motion of the earth would leave the moon behind. Galileo, however, discovered satellites to Jupiter that revolved around that planet while it in turn revolved around the sun; if Jupiter's satellites stayed with that planet, then our moon could stay with us as *we* revolved around the sun.

It seemed to Tycho that while the Ptolemaic system was too complicated, the Copernican, although containing nothing contrary to mathematical principles, yet infringed on those of physics, as the heavy and sluggish earth would seem unfit to move; furthermore, the system was opposed to Scripture. Tycho could scarcely be called a particularly religious man, but he felt that the motion of the earth must somehow be reconciled to

[12] Copernicus' conclusions, as described in his famous book *De revolutionibus orbium coelestium,* were that the sun was the center of the universe, the earth only a planet like Mars, and it and all the planets revolved about the sun. Modern astronomy has been based upon this system.

[94]

certain passages in the Bible. Moses, he thought, must have known astronomy since he called the moon the lesser light, though the sun and moon were apparently of equal size, and the prophets, he felt, must have known more about astronomy than did other people of their time.

Copernicus adopted the earth's rotation, which Ptolemy rejected, and Tycho agreed with Ptolemy; Copernicus adopted sun-centered motion for all planets, whereas Ptolemy insisted that all planets revolved around the earth, and Tycho said moon and sun revolved around the earth, while all others revolved around the sun, truly a mixture of old and new. Professor J. L. E. Dreyer in his book on Tycho Brahe gives the following as Tycho's theory of planetary motion. It was one that seemed to him to accord with mathematical and physical principles and that at the same time did not incur the censure of theologians—as had poor Galileo's.

"The earth was the center of the universe, and the center of the orbits of the sun and the moon, as well as of the sphere of the fixed stars, which latter revolved around it in twenty-four hours, carrying all the planets with it. The sun was the center of the five planets, of which Mercury and Venus move in orbits whose radii are smaller than that of the solar orbit, while the orbits of Mars, Jupiter and Saturn encircle the earth.

"This system accounts for the irregularities in the planetary motions, which the ancients explained by epicycles and Copernicus by the annual motion of the earth, and it shows why the solar motion is mixed up in all the planetary theories. The remaining inequalities, which formerly were explained by the eccentric circle and the deferent, and by Copernicus by epicycles moving in eccentric circles, could also, in the new hypotheses, be explained in a similar way. . . .

"It fell to Kepler, after many years of indefatigable work, to deduct from the observations made at Hveen, the three Kepler laws, which swept away the last traces of the old, artificial combination of circles and made the planetary system clear and simple. . . . Though Tycho Brahe did not live long enough to

[95]

draw the important conclusions from his observations, he had more than a suspicion that the secrets of the planetary system might be bared by his observations."

It must be noted that there was one redeeming feature in Tycho's adoption of a spurious scheme. He was able to make very good observations for parallax. He reasoned that if the earth revolved around the sun, he would view the stars from two positions, separated by a considerable distance, at intervals of six months. He determined that, if this were true, the distance of the stars must be at least 4,000 times the distance of the sun (by the method of parallax and his smallest reading of his instruments); this would put the nearest star far beyond the most distant planet, Saturn, only ten times as far from the sun as the earth; this tremendous space between the orbit of Saturn and the sphere of the fixed stars was, in Tycho's mind, a sign of wastefulness on the part of the Creator, and this he would not admit. Therefore the earth could not be moving from one place to another. In other words, he used his observational technique to give evidence, albeit inadequate, for a system differing from the Copernican. Not until 1837 were the observations made that he was trying to make—i.e., actual detection of the parallax of a star.

Today, the Copernican theory can be proved in several independent ways, some of them yielding numerical values for the earth's speed in its orbit, and they all agree. It is no longer a hypothesis; it is an established law of nature.

CHAPTER SIX

*When the morning stars sang to-
gether, and all the sons of God shouted
for joy. . . .*—JOB 38:7

YCHO's duties as a court officer, as a nobleman and as a property owner did not permit him, as he would have preferred, to spend all his nights and days on Hveen. He was obliged to interrupt his work and to attend King Frederik, first at Odense in the island of Funen with many other nobles, when the Dukes of Holstein were given the Duchy and the island of Femern in fief, and then his presence was likewise required at Lund, with the rest of the Scania nobles, to swear fealty to the young heir apparent, Christian.

Returning to Hveen he received the sad news that his devoted uncle, Steen Bille, who had always befriended him and stood up for him, who had been like a father to him ever since Otto and Jørgen Brahe passed away, had died at Herrevad. Naturally Tycho wished to hurry to the place where he had first gazed upon "his" star and follow the devoted friend to his last resting-place. He was scarcely back at his work again when he was informed that his brother, Knud, the justice of the peace at Bygholm, near Horsens in Jutland had been, to put it mildly, misbehaving with a noblewoman, and had been forced to flee abroad. However, none of these state and family matters interested him as much as the lunar eclipse in 1580 or his own definition of the planetary system.

Then again, the idea of possessing a printing press became such an obsession with him that finally, in 1584, he decided to prepare a little nearby building to house one of his own. Three things were needed to begin work: a printer, presses with type and accessories, and the best paper he could purchase. All would have to come from Germany, for the Danish supply of any of them was exceedingly scanty. He was lucky in his first printer, Christopher Weida, for he was conscientious, accurate, hard-working and unusually well-versed in his craft. Vedel was naturally one of the first to whom Tycho confided his new venture, writing to him that he proposed setting up a small printing establishment of his own at Uraniborg, that he had engaged a printer, and that he hoped to obtain much of the equipment needed at the next Frankfurt fair. He also wrote his good friend, Professor Heinrich Brucæus of Rostock, with whom he constantly corresponded on literary matters, that he had sent for presses, types and other requisites, and asked him to help obtain various essential materials. Tycho also stated that he had been working on a book about comets as well as the new star, and found he could not get it printed in Copenhagen, owing to the plague that had broken out there, and that such printers as there were, who were not stricken, had their hands full of uninteresting books and pamphlets. He was therefore, he wrote, going to do his own printing and was sending his man Joachim to Wittenberg to buy both presses and paper, though he realized it was not so easy to procure what he wished.

His restless energy overcame all obstacles, so that the following year, early in 1585, simple presses were installed and printing commenced in the little building to the south of the castle. Tycho could now proudly write his highly valued friend Henrik Rantzau, the Governor of Holstein, and offer "to print anything for him which he desired," and add that he would shortly send him some specimens of his work. This he did by forwarding him the Latin poems he had composed at the deaths of Pratensis and Hans Frandsen, as well as others to Falk Gjøe and Niels Kaas.

At the start, at least, Tycho's printer had little ornamental material and only a few of the capitals in the favorite styles of the period, and he employed few cartouches or framed titles. But he had a quantity of illustrations, reproductions of buildings and instruments, some of them depicted as mathematical or astronomical figures. Tycho used two kinds of type, one for his text, and a second, somewhat larger one, for titles and headings. For his Latin text he used also several larger and smaller sizes of type, both roman and italic. It is quite inconceivable how he had time to go into all such details with the eyes of an expert. But then—he was Tycho Brahe.

Armilla from Stjerneborg

Portrait of King Christian IV of Denmark
(1588-1648)

Everything ready, he was wildly impatient to start his first printing on the excellent paper that after endless difficulties had just arrived from the Mecklenburg mills of Grabow and Neustadt—fourteen to fifteen bales of both writing and printing paper, a huge quantity for those days.

The poems having been printed, woodcuts were made of Uraniborg (in 1585) and its most important instruments, and prints of these followed the poems to various Danish and German friends. When some distinguished person or friend visited him, Tycho was in fact to hand him as a parting souvenir a poem of his own composition and printing, generally accompanied by a woodcut of Uraniborg.

Calendars were greatly appreciated in Tycho's day,[1] and not only by the king but by the people at large, for they offered much useful and necessary advice by which to regulate your life. The doctor or barber might be far away and unable to bleed or to dose you, but the calendar was there, right at hand, to inform you how to meet each emergency. It told you when and where to go to market, what was the day of the week and the year, how to act when your dog or your child was ill, or a cartwheel broken down, how pregnant women must under no circumstances be sighted by a wolf, how to differentiate in the treatment of a sick son or daughter, what to do when fruit trees or wives stopped bearing, or a prolonged drought threatened the crops. Astrology, experience and genuine wisdom all aided the compilers of the calendars.

The first Uraniborg booklet was a calendar for the coming year of 1587,[2] containing astrological and meteorological data as well as reports on the comet that had been observed by Tycho in 1585. The little work was dedicated to Prince Christian (later, King Christian IV) and was in reality more or less of a diary compiled by the pupil Elias Olsen Cimber (also called Morsing).[3] It was published under the title *Diarium astrologicum et meteorologicum.*[4]

[1] Nicholas Helvaderus sent thousands of almanacs with their "prognostica" all over Germany and, like Tycho, kept a meteorological diary.

[2] The year in which Mary, Queen of Scots, was beheaded.

[3] The Latinized form often used is Elias Olai Cimber.   [4] See Bibliography.

[101]

Tycho's pupil, Petrus Fischer, was permitted to issue shortly afterwards under his master's guidance a wall calendar for King Christian[5] in which was announced that when the sun entered Virgo, namely, on August 14, then one might make friends with a maid, but nothing more; one must take good medicine, cut the cloth for garments, buy and sell and get one's corn to the miller. When the sun entered Libra, a month later, then was the time to wander abroad, cut one's hair, enter into matrimony, seed and plant and be bled, except in the loins. The information given on one of Tycho's calendars included a listing of the days, thirty-two in all, on which it was highly inadvisable to give birth to children, to be married, to be taken ill, to move from one household to another, to loaf about the streets, to buy or sell or go to the courthouse. If you wished good luck, you were to break off a branch of your cherry tree on St. Barbara's day and put it in a glass, daily giving it fresh water, which would keep it flowering until Christmas day.

As soon as the printing establishment was in full swing, Tycho wrote King Frederik all about it and, always wishing to be helpful, Frederik issued an order: "That our man and servant Tyge Brahe of Knudstrup, must be given as many *Cartas Cosmographicas* or as much paper as is to be found in our library in our castle of Copenhagen or in our Danish or Norwegian kingdoms or in any of our possessions, so as to aid him in the undertaking which he has written us about."

Tycho had evidently stressed what a hard time he was having in obtaining the necessary paper, and King Frederik in his regal manner had replied by giving his mathematician a "blanket" order. The king looked upon Tycho not only as a great man but as a confidential servant to whom he could turn for advice. Wishing to express his appreciation, he presented him, at this time, with the insignia of the Elephant, which also carried the king's initials, suspended from several golden chains. This was not as yet a decoration conferring knighthood, and did not be-

[5] Frederik died in 1588 and was succeeded by his son Christian IV. He was a minor at the time, so a regency was established.

come so until the time of Christian V, in 1693. Tycho was never knighted and thus entitled to be called "Herr," but was merely a "Junker" or Squire. Tycho invariably wore his Elephant around his neck and was immensely proud of it.

One learns to know Tycho best through his letters, for they give a clear picture of his character and personality as well as of the vast scope of his reading and wisdom in many matters outside his science. Letter-writing was very much the habit and fashion of the day, and Tycho employed his favorite apprentices as postmen, sending them back and forth across Europe.[6]

Except for an occasional courier or visitor, letters were about the only means of receiving family, court or international news. When we pick up Tycho's correspondence, we find it filled with the strangest hodgepodge of events—the state of Her Majesty's pregnancy, the appearance of the last comet or philosophical book, the killing of a pig or the punishment of a peasant. The variety of subjects treated is illustrated by the following extracts from letters written and received by him. Tycho writes: "In passing I will also mention that I have taken considerable interest in chemical mixtures [compounds] and experiments, owing to the fact that the substances treated are analogous to the celestial system and influence.[7] I therefore generally refer to them as the astronomy of the earth. As I, ever since I was twenty-three, have made such investigations, in addition to my celestial observations, I have made quite a few experiments with metals and minerals, as well as with precious stones and herbs and other substances. In such matters I should like to get in touch with distinguished and noble persons, as well as with other prominent and learned men, busied with such matters and having knowledge of them, and occasionally to report to them one thing or another, if I only might feel certain that they would keep it secret. For to do so for the benefit of the

[6] While most of his extant letters are to be found in the Vienna Library, ninety-eight of them are listed as in that of Basel.

[7] Tycho refers, for instance, to quicksilver as corresponding to the planet Mercury, lead to Saturn, etc.

public is neither reasonable nor profitable. For while many pretend to have knowledge of such things, everyone cannot experiment harmlessly with such mysteries, in the right manner and according to the laws of nature."

His learned German friend, the Landgrave William, sends the following note: "Yesterday, God and my wife blessed me with a son. I cannot send you the comet observations which you believe I have made, for I did not make them. My restless daughter Caroline is to be married on October thirteenth and I am obtaining much wine for the event, so the bridegroom has much to look forward to."

Again, the landgrave writes him, asking Tycho if he could not possibly procure him a strange animal, which Tycho took for an elk, from his Swedish estate or Norwegian fief. After considerable effort Tycho finally obtained what he believed to be the desired beast, but *en route* to the landgrave's property it stopped over at Landskrona Castle with Tycho's nephew. There it unfortunately walked up the great stone staircase to the buttery where servants gave it so much strong beer that when it descended to the courtyard it lost its footing, broke a leg, and had to be shot.[8] Tycho wrote at length about the accident, coupling it with news concerning the young king's education. The landgrave's note in reply shows a marvelous jumble of various languages. Commenting upon the sad state of affairs in France he writes, *"dass es misserimus status totius Europae ist."*

Despite the fact that most of the letters were written by his pupils and merely signed by him, it is inconceivable how Tycho found time to keep up his vast correspondence amidst his many other varied and exacting occupations. At one time he was corresponding with no less than eighty-five persons. Day by day, out went his letters to Vedel, Craig, Wolf, Dancey, the Hainzels, Johannes Major, Holger Rosencrantz, Chytræus,

[8] Wilhelm Nordlind, *Ur Tycho Brahes Brevväxling* . . . , 1926, p. 139. See Bibliography.

Buchanan, Scultetus, Bongarcius (Jacques Bongars), Pratensis, Hagecius, Brucæus, Rantzau, Magini, Seccerwitz, Sturtz, Longomontanus, Tengnagel, Herwarto of Hohenheim, Peucer, Scaliger, Bachmeister, Brasch, the landgrave or his astronomer, Christopher Rothmann. The letters generally inquire about some book or instrument or star or comet, but again, at times, they contain amusing little sidelights on the days and on varied matters passing through the writer's astonishing mind and lively imagination.

His two principal correspondents were the landgrave, William of Hesse[9] and the governor of Holstein, Henrik Rantzau. The correspondence pretty generally dealt with astronomical matters, but at times touched on mutual courtesies or the political situation. Tycho was bitterly disappointed that the landgrave, on account of King Frederik's death, was forced to abandon a projected trip to a meeting of the Danish nobility[10] in Copenhagen that he had promised to combine with a long-intended stay at Uraniborg. When the landgrave wrote during the early days of the regency and inquired of Tycho about the Danish Government, the latter replied: "Your Grace wishes to know about conditions in Denmark, the land of your forefathers. During this temporary government the country is comparatively happy and tranquil. Our most gracious Prince and chosen King grows daily, not only in years and bodily strength, but also in virtue and knowledge, which I value even more. We have thus the firm hope, that he will in time follow in the heroic footsteps of his virtuous and highly praiseworthy father and will be fitted to head the Government creditably. He seems as though born to it, and it seems as if God intended him to replace his most praiseworthy father, who was taken from us all too soon. In the meanwhile, during the time the young Prince is under age, the four senior councilors are in charge of the Government. The principal one is Niels Kaas, a

---

[9] The correspondence with the landgrave was published at Uraniborg in 1596. See Bibliography.
[10] *Herredag.*

[105]

man who in addition to his ancient nobility, must be praised for his experience, industry and great wisdom. He is also much at home among books and diplomacy. If anything particularly difficult or important arises, then it is referred to the meeting of the nobility [*Herredag*], called once a year in midsummer, or to the entire Crown Council which is summoned if necessary, before its usual convocation. Our Government is thus a kind of Aristocracy [oligarchy]—which form is not so bad—until our most gracious, elected King comes of age.

"Everything in the meanwhile proceeds decently and well, and full of respect for our Prince. May God continue to bless us, so that everything may continue peaceably and happily, and may He protect our most desirable Prince, and uphold him in the chosen path of virtue."

Tycho often heard of the expected arrival in Denmark of some distinguished foreigner whom according to his custom he felt he must see before his departure. Such a visitor was the historian, Daniel Rogers, who arrived to negotiate matters relating to the Sound duties and the seizure of English vessels. Tycho wished through him to beg Queen Elizabeth's copyright for his books in England. Lord Willoughby d'Eresby arrived as the queen's envoy with the Order of the Garter for King Frederik and for consultations with him on matters of national import, after which he sailed over to Hveen. Many another came and went, calling at Hveen en route.

Though he lived and ruled like a prince on his island, it had come to be very far from the quiet and secluded spot Tycho had imagined. While it had seemed idyllic, near enough to the capital to obtain books or instruments or scholarly advice, and yet far from the world he did not wish to have pestering him, it proved, in fact, to be so near to Copenhagen as to bring a steady stream of visitors. Some came out of legitimate scientific interest to talk with the sage or see his marvelous instruments, others out of idle curiosity, attracted by his great name.

Queen Sophia came on June 27, 1586, to honor him as Denmark's most distinguished scientist, and because she herself was interested in various matters on which Tycho was working. She hoped particularly that his chemical experiments might lead to the long-sought discovery of how to make gold. Though she was obliged to remain for three days on account of a storm, she did not outstay her welcome, but had such a good time that she stated she would soon be back and bring her Mecklenburg parents with her. She added that she was filled with joy and wonder at all she saw, for "the like has never been found or seen anywhere since the creation of the world, nor has anything been read or seen or known about such marvelous instruments."

On the occasion of the visit Tycho was able to do his friend Vedel a good turn by informing the queen of the collection of old Danish ballads he had been making, which she promptly offered to have published on Vedel's own press. This gave Tycho the greatest pleasure.

Tycho was also able to welcome the great Jacob Curtius, Emperor Rudolph's vice-chancellor, and his youthful correspondent, Christopher Rothmann, Landgrave William of Hesse's astronomer, with whom he had many heated arguments about the Copernican system.

During his reign, Frederik II had attempted much for the benefit of his kingdom, but he accomplished nothing which redounded more to its glory and renown than his protection of and assistance to Tycho Brahe. That he had really understood him and was free from the intolerance of his age was astonishing. Shortly before his death, in writing to a friend King Frederik testified handsomely to Tycho's services. "He was," wrote the king, "a faithful servant and friend. He executed conscientiously that for which originally he had been employed. He cast dependable horoscopes for all my sons and gave me notice throughout my life as to all heavenly portents sent by God Almighty to warn me and my kingdoms."

The king's work was now over and when he died on April 4, 1588, just as Tycho was about to leave on a visit to the Landgrave of Hesse, Tycho lost his best friend. Just four years before, to a day, when Tycho observed the eclipse of the sun, he had announced that this day foreboded some coming evil.

Vedel, as court chaplain, gave the lengthy, tedious funeral oration, in which, with the strange frankness of the day, after reciting the late king's many virtues and good deeds, he stated: "If His Grace could have kept from the injurious drink, which is much too prevalent all over the world among princes and nobles and common people, then it would seem to human eyes and understanding that he might have lived for many years to come." None of the bereaved found this reflection either out of place or strange—nor probably did any of them take warning.

Tycho's good friend the chancellor, Niels Kaas, in writing to Valkendorf informed him that immediately previous to the king's death they attended Duke Hans's wedding at Sønderborg where His Majesty "had become weak from drink; he had likewise drunk deeply the next day and Sunday also, as there was not much else to do. He had finally consented to take a little medicine, but his stomach was very miserable."

Now that King Frederik was gone, Tycho fully realized that a change might soon come in the good fortune of bygone years. Added to the disaster of the king's death, Tycho was aware that he had recently been spending huge sums on his new instruments, and how would the new administration view that matter? He very sensibly decided to make a clean breast of it; in fact, there was no way out of it, for payments were due. So he sent word to the councilors that he was in immediate need of six thousand daler, a very large sum for those days. As King Christian was only eleven years old at his father's death, a regency had been appointed consisting of four of Denmark's most powerful and capable noblemen—the chancellor of the realm, Niels Kaas, the chancellor of the exchequer, Christofer Valkendorf, Admiral Peder Munk, and the governor of Jutland, Jørgen Rosenkrantz.

Tycho had constantly been uneasy about the final disposition of Uraniborg. He had merely been given it as a fief for life and, the legitimacy of his sons being questioned, they would probably be unable to retain it when he himself passed away. Tycho consequently had Vedel draft a document whereby Hveen would be declared not merely a fief which would revert to the Crown at his death, but a great Danish observatory in perpetuity, so that his sons might continue their astronomical work there throughout their lives. But the time never came when Tycho felt he could present this document to the councilors with any chance of its approval.

In reply to the "memorial" that Tycho had forwarded recounting his financial troubles, Kaas and Rosenkrantz came to Hveen to look it over and see what was going on there, and on their return advised the privy council to pay over the money and to promise to keep Uraniborg and its buildings in repair. They even went further, in recommending that Tycho retain his Norwegian Nordfjord fief. And finally, so as to facilitate his work whenever he was in Copenhagen, he was given two houses in Farvergade (the Street of the Dyers) and a lean-to, near some property belonging to the king, and the burgomaster was instructed to lend him for his observations, when desired, a stone tower by the city walls "and a small piece of the ramparts, as far as the fence." The houses, being next to one of Tycho's own, were a most welcome gift, the only obligation on his part being that of providing quarters for the former occupant, the dyer. His most pressing debts off his mind, Tycho felt he could at last turn to the publication of his first great book, an idea which he had been cherishing for years.

The contents of the book were in his mind or among his notes; the presses, printer and printer's devils were there. The only difficulty lay in the everlasting lack of paper. Tycho found that there was practically none for sale in Denmark, and he knew from earlier experience, even with the little he had needed, that it was difficult and tedious to procure it from his own country's only mill. But nothing daunted Tycho. The best way out of the difficulty was to build a paper mill of his own, just as he had a printing press. When last in Germany he had visited various paper mills, and had he not years back set up one with his Uncle Steen at Herrevad? Power was obtained from the water of the fishponds, which were dammed up and connected so that they easily turned a mill wheel. The entire construction went up as if by magic. On the wall of the little building Tycho cut in Latin:

THIS WALL AND THIS PAPER MILL, WITH ALL THE NECESSARY ARRANGEMENTS, AS WELL AS THE UPPER FISHPOND, HAVE BEEN BUILT WHERE NOTHING PREVIOUSLY EXISTED, BY TYCHO BRAHE, O. [OTTOSØN] OF KNUDSTRUP, OUT OF HIS OWN RESOURCES, FOR THE USE OF HIS NATIVE COUNTRY, HIMSELF, AND POSTERITY.

BEGUN 1590 — COMPLETED 1591
LET US WORK AS LONG AS THERE IS TIME.

Experienced workmen were, as usual, obtained from Germany, and proper influence was exerted in the right places. "Rag Sermons" were preached in various churches exhorting the congregations, for the public good, to furnish the useful Hveen paper mill with its needed raw materials. The appeal proved a success. The paper produced at home was not, it is true, as good as the best made in Germany, but it was Tycho's own, with his watermarks of Uraniborg and the Brahe arms, and there was plenty of it and no need of any longer being haunted by the fear of having to stop the presses because the supply from the Duke of Mecklenburg's mills had given out.

Tycho had long had in mind the idea of compiling all his astronomic observations and publishing them in several volumes to be entitled *Astronomiæ instauratæ progymnasmata. De mundi ætherii recentioribus phænomenis.* The great day at last arrived when he handed his printer, Christopher Weida, what was intended as the second volume of the work,

De mundi ætherii recentioribus phænomenis, which appeared in a 238-page quarto "Uraniburgum, 1588."[11] Its ten chapters, following the usual elaborate introduction, dealt mainly with Tycho's observations of the 1577 comet, which he had first caught sight of one evening when he was out fishing in one of his ponds. He demonstrated that the comet, from its insensible parallax, was no terrestrial exhalation, as commonly supposed, but a body traversing planetary space, and not, as usually considered, a sign of divine punishment or a portent of coming evil, originating in the earth or air. The book further contained remarks on the 1572 star (Nova stella), on the movements of the moon and methods of determining the position of the fixed stars. There was also a chapter on Tycho's plan of the cosmos, and much of his research, up to then, on the motion of the sun and on refraction and precession.

The edition was small, yet large enough to give Tycho the infinite satisfaction of sending copies of it to his closest friends and those he valued most in the field of science. As the book became known throughout the learned world it did much to draw attention to the remarkable work that was being done at Uraniborg, work that rested not only on a broad foundation, but on many entirely new discoveries and conclusions.

Tycho never lived to see either a completed first or third volume to his *New Astronomy* published. New thoughts and matters, which he wished to place in the first volume, were constantly arising throughout what was left of his life. Death overtook him, and it remained for his great pupil Johan Kepler to continue it in Prague.[12]

[11] See Bibliography.

[12] A portion of the first volume of *Progymnasmata* was printed in 1590, though the whole work was not completed until after Tycho's death in 1601. It described solar and lunar observations, as well as "the new star." The third volume was to contain descriptions of the comets that appeared in 1580, 1582, 1590, 1593, and 1596; and much of the other material that had been put together never appeared until 1845.

During the years 1588-1592 Tycho did considerable work on the first volume and though it was incomplete, he sent copies of the finished portions of the book to a few selected friends.

Among the earlier publications of the Uraniborg press were also several that fortunately give us, either in woodcuts or engravings, excellent pictures of Tycho and Uraniborg. Aided by contemporary descriptions, these give a good idea of the astronomer. No one could have looked at him without being more or less hypnotized by his nose, made of an alloy of gold and silver and painted to resemble as far as possible a flesh tint. It must have been almost repulsive.

Otherwise, he looked typically Danish, and of a type that has persevered—high coloring, reddish-yellow hair, and a stocky, burly middle-sized frame. We are told that the dwarf Jeppe's sole useful employment, in which he had been drilled, was to cut his master's hair. This he was commanded to do sparingly, so as to hide his master's incipient baldness. Tycho attempted to conceal this partially by brushing his hair forward, over the forehead. But Jeppe was never allowed to touch the elegant, pointed beard and the very long, flowing moustaches. Tycho had the general commanding presence of a great nobleman who knew his own mind, and was used to giving orders and having them obeyed. His pictures show him in the Elizabethan costume of the day,[13] doublet and silk-lined cape, high collar and uncomfortable, piped, white ruff around his neck. He wore rings on almost all his fingers, and on his breast two rows of heavy gold chains, one group carrying the Elephant, the other a medallion with the picture of Christian IV. Tycho's head is usually shown covered by a puffed hat with a jaunty plume on one side, such as might have been worn by Sir Walter Raleigh or the Duc de Guise.

We know of only three original, contemporaneous pictures of Tycho. The best of these is a woodcut made by Gemperlin when Tycho was forty, from which in turn Geyn made an engraving with a few changes. The second was a painting also by Gemperlin, which unfortunately burned up with many other historical treasures in the Fredriksborg Castle fire of 1859. An engraving

[13] See Frontispiece.

of this had been made before it burned. The third is in the Edinburgh Observatory. There are a great many other paintings and engravings, some eighty-seven in all, the best of them in the *Collectio Langertiana* in Scania, and in Karen Brahe's cloister in Odense, which has a fine copy of the burned Gemperlin portrait.

Tycho's explosive, enthusiastic, uncontrolled character belonged entirely to the sixteenth century. He was a child of nature as well as a child of genius, of a dynamic character with the faults which usually accompany his type, so sure of what he was accomplishing that he not only dominated but domineered. He was a great scholar but not a student of humanity. Though he became the most famous scientist of his day, he also became too expensive a royal luxury, be it for Emperor Rudolph or King Christian. He was an egocentric, except when alone in the night with the stars, where he felt humble in spirit before the majesty of the heavens. He was eager and zealous, insatiable in the search for scientific truth, yet he possessed great facility for friendship among his peers, drawing to him men of his ilk. In Denmark, as also in a large part of Germany, he was considered the great astronomical, medical and chemical authority of his day, and learned persons of the time were often referred to as "being as wise as Tycho Brahe." Having freed himself once and for all of the superstitions of his day and generation, he recognized in Hveen no authority except experience. He had traveled far from his university lessons where he had been taught that everything rested on authority, be it religious belief, natural science or the lessons of the past.

CHAPTER SEVEN

Praise ye the Lord. . . . Praise ye him, sun and moon: praise him, all ye stars of light.—PSALM 148:1-3

Portrait of Tycho Brahe

Portrait of Tycho Brahe, with the Brahe Arms

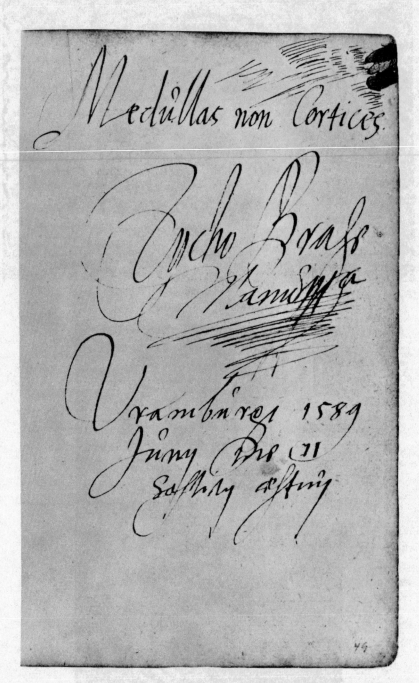

Tycho Brahe's Autograph

T the time Tycho was finishing his great book, the fourteen-year-old Christian IV's curiosity to see Uraniborg, about which he had always heard so much, became so great that he finally prevailed upon Christofer Valkendorf, Admiral Peder Munk, Jørgen Rosenkrantz, and his tutor, Hak Ulfstand, to take him to Hveen.

The news of the royal visit naturally called forth considerable excitement on Hveen, and great preparations were soon afoot. Tycho rightly felt the importance for the future of making a favorable impression upon the king and the three powerful regents, two of whom were dependable old friends, though the attitude of the third, Valkendorf, was very doubtful. The royal party was greeted at the landing, and a tour of inspection followed. Then Christian and Tycho settled down in the library to discuss, over their silver goblets, fortifications and Christian's hobby of shipbuilding, and the possibility of Tycho accepting a few additional students who had already learned the rudiments of mathematics and astronomy and instructing them in whatever might prove useful for shipbuilding. The king having admired among the instruments he had seen a brass globe that, by means of internal cog-wheels, imitated the diurnal motion of the heavens, the rising and setting of the sun, and the phases of the moon, Tycho handed him this as a souvenir of his visit, and the royal lad, not to be outdone, took the gold chain carrying his likeness from around his neck, and hung it around Tycho's beside his "Elephant."

On Christian's return to his Copenhagen palace, his tutor gave him as his Latin exercise for the next morning the task of writing a full description of the Hveen visit.

Other scarcely less magnificent visitors soon followed the king, upsetting the steady work and equilibrium of the little island. Early in 1590 came one whose visit caused almost as great a commotion as King Christian's amid the sextants and globes of Hveen, namely, the son of Mary, Queen of Scots— James VI of Scotland, later James I of England. He had first sought the hand of Elizabeth of Denmark, but Queen Elizabeth of England, who got wind of the matter, realized the importance of the Danish Navy and felt this was altogether too good a match for her tiresome northern neighbor. She put her foot down, frustrated James's plan, and Princess Elizabeth was quietly affianced to the Duke of Brunswick. However pedantic and boring James may have been, he was at least persistent, and this time both secretive and discreet in his plans. Letting no news escape from Edinburgh Castle, he sent his Earl Marshal, Lord Keith, to Denmark (1589) to seek the hand of the second sister, Princess Anne. His embassy was crowned with success, for the marriage was celebrated by proxy shortly after Keith's arrival in Denmark, at the newly constructed castle of Kronborg, whereupon Anne started for Scotland, accompanied by Peder Munk, Steen Brahe and Breide Rantzau.

Fourteen vessels and a large retinue sailed north from Copenhagen to join King James. Unfortunately it took some time for the lovers to meet, for evil forces, more formidable than the English, seemed arrayed against the match. Several Danish witches—like all witches lighter than water and consequently unable to swim—swooped down on their broomsticks upon the helms of the vessels, and badly retarded their progress and "by diabolical methods infuriated the waves." One storm after another swept the Sound and the Kattegat, and the princess failed to arrive where the lover waited impatiently for her.

After several weeks of anxious maneuvering Anne and her seasick and terrified ladies and noblemen put in at Oslo, where she lodged with the head of the Shoemakers' Guild. In Copenhagen one of the greatest witch trials ever held was forthwith assembled. Clergymen, professors and astrologers were summoned from far and near. One after another the witches were dragged from their foul hiding places, their confessions extracted and their burning decreed. In this Tycho took no part, probably having excused himself owing to the pressure of work at Hveen.[1]

King James waited, wondering whether Queen Elizabeth's envious policy which opposed his forming any matrimonial alliance, would once more balk his Danish plans. He was of a naturally timorous disposition, and not fond of adventurous exploits. This time, however, as soon as he had news of what had happened, he resolved to brave every danger rather than have his desire to consummate his marriage to the Danish princess frustrated. So, despite the late season, the tempestuous North Sea, and a vessel ill fitted for the voyage, he sailed for Norway and arrived safely at the Oslo shoemaker's.

The wedding was solemnized at Akershus Castle by the Royal Chaplain, David Lyndsay, on November 25, 1589. In front of the royal coach, despite the freezing cold, danced four naked negro boys to honor the queen. All four of them died of pneumonia and followed the witches to another world.

After the wedding James rejoiced to receive an invitation from the dowager Queen Sophia to come with his bride for a visit in Copenhagen before returning to Scotland. The Norwegian officials present at the ceremonies cared little about this, but a great deal about their Shetland and Orkney Isles which the Danish councilors were giving James in lieu of any other dower from Anne. The newly married couple were given a rousing welcome in Denmark. James's wobbly legs were tied to his saddle and around the belly of his horse so as to enable him to join the daily hunt, and in the evenings king and noblemen were carried to their beds by their pages.

Priding himself upon his scholarly attainments and scientific

[1] As late as 1603 a law was enacted in England "against those making invocation or conjuration of any evil or wicked spirit, or taking up any dead person with view of employing him or her in sorcery or practicing witchcraft." King James himself wrote a treatise on witchcraft. Did he have in mind particularly those witches that delayed his bride? The witch trials in Scotland lasted until the eighteenth century.

knowledge, James asked one day to be taken to Hveen to see the wonderful castle and instruments of the great Tycho Brahe. The company rode to Elsinore, whence they went by boat to Hveen to spend the day with the astronomer. Long and learned discussions were held between the king and his host relating to the motion Copernicus had ascribed to the earth and, after the elaborate luncheon was over, all the wonders of Uraniborg and Stjerneborg with their various instruments and installations were shown and explained to the monarch. He was delighted when he discovered in the library a portrait of his former teacher, George Buchanan, so pleased indeed that he readily complied with Tycho's request for a copyright for his writings in Scotland, as well as with the request that some tin and lead be sent to Hveen when he returned home. But that was not all. In one of the astronomer's prized leaflets he wrote:

> *Anno 1590, XX Martii*
> *Est nobilis ira Leonis*
> *Parcere subjectis et debellare superbos*[2]
> *Jacobus Rex*

as well as the following verse:

> *Qua temere est ausus Phæton vel præstat Apollo*
> *Qui regit ignivomos Æthere anhelus equos.*
> *Plus Tycho, cuncta astra regis; tibi cedit Apollo*
> *Charus & Uraniæ es hospes, alumnus, amor.*[3]

And as a further reminder of his visit he left behind him as a final token of his favor two of his finest mastiffs.

In forwarding Tycho the official letter granting the Scottish copyright, James wrote: "Nor have I become acquainted with

---

[2] "20th March, 1590,
   The Lion's wrath is not ignoble
   Spare the conquered; overthrow the haughty." (*Danske Magazin*, ii, p. 266.)
[3] What Phaeton dared was by Apollo done
   Who ruled the fiery horses of the sun.
   More Tycho doth, he rules the stars above
   And is Urania's favorite and love.

these things [astronomical matters] only from the relation of others, or from a bare inspection of your works, but I have seen them before my own eyes, and have heard them with my own ears in your residence at Uraniborg, and have drawn them from various learned and agreeable conversations which I there held with you, and which even now affect my mind to such a degree that it is difficult to determine whether I recollect them with greater pleasure or admiration, as I now willingly testify by this license to present to future generations. . . ."

Shortly afterwards Duke Henry Julius of Brunswick arrived at Hveen; he had married James's first choice, Princess Elizabeth. After Tycho had entertained his visitor, the latter, with considerably less modesty than was displayed by King Christian, did not wait until offered a souvenir, but stated boldly that he would like a small revolving statue of Mercury that he had noticed on the roof of Stjerneborg, and which Tycho did not at all want to part with. Still, a brother-in-law of the king could not be offended, so Mercury was removed from his airy perch and handed to the duke on condition that he would copy it and return the original. As the duke did not live up to his side of the bargain, Tycho at a later date retaliated by ordering the anecdote inserted in a printed description of Uraniborg.

There is no question that the instruments caused the greatest excitement of all the wonders shown the guests, for, though crowned heads were obliged to restrain the exhibition of their feelings, we read that when the otherwise staid and sober mathematician, Paul Wittich from Breslau, first saw some of the instruments, "he jumped with joy." Prince William of Courland, the English envoy, Duncan Liddel, and the Duke and Duchess of Mecklenburg, accompanied by their daughter, followed suit in visiting Hveen, and Tycho then felt he had more than enough of great folk. There was, however, one guest whom it gave him particular satisfaction to welcome, and that was the landgrave's mathematician, Christopher Rothmann, with whom he had much to talk over.

Foreigners as well as Danes arrived from far and wide, drawn by other motives than curiosity or a love of astronomy. Frequently they came to obtain medicaments for their various ailments. These Tycho distributed freely to the rage of physicians, from the "Court Medicus," Peder Severinus (Peder Sørensen) down to humbler practitioners, who averred that the astronomer was stealing their business. Their complaints against this distinguished practitioner seem to have been governed by nothing more than an audacious and mean-spirited envy, when one considers that in the entire kingdom there were only twelve physicians, the principal "curing" being within the province of the barbers. Among the crucibles and retorts of his chemical laboratory it was reported that Tycho concocted cures for almost every ailment, and that he dispensed his salves, syrups and powders with both kindness and interest. As he could concoct cures for almost every ill, the more ignorant whispered that he was probably a magician.

It is interesting to note his own remarks on the subject of alchemy. "On consideration and by the advice of the most learned men," he wrote, "I thought it improper to unfold the secrets of the art [of alchemy] to the vulgar, as few persons are capable of using its mysteries to advantage and without detriment." Tycho was not a believer in the medical dogmas of the alchemist of his day, but he did believe he was the discoverer of a new elixir, which went by his name and which later came to be sold by almost every apothecary as a specific against the epidemic diseases that were then ravaging Germany. Even Emperor Rudolph used it as a preventative. Its basis was Venice treacle (theriaca Andromachi). In advising the emperor how to use it, Tycho wrote:[4] "When properly prepared it is better than gold. It may be made still more valuable by mixing with it a single scruple either of gold, tincture of corals, or sapphire, or garnet, or solution of pearls, or of potable gold, if this can be obtained free of all corrosive matter. In order to render the

[4] J. L. E. Dreyer, *Tycho Brahe* . . . , p. 130.

medicine helpful for all diseases which can be cured by perspiration, and which constitute a third of those which attack the
human frame, it should be combined with antimony."

Tycho's letters of this period show plainly his increasing fear
and uncertainty as to the future. Though he still had powerful
friends in the Crown Council, his great protector was no longer
there to ward off blows directed against him. True enough, after
King Frederik's death, the four regents had declared "they
would endeavor according to their best ability to urge the continuation of the previous astronomical work on Hveen and try
to induce the King, when of age, to allocate certain revenues
for the scientific work on Hveen." But Tycho put little faith in
this. After his two powerful friends Kaas and Rosenkrantz had
followed their master to the grave, and his brother Steen had
proved without influence as a councilor, Tycho began putting
out feelers abroad to ascertain what assistance there might be,
were he ever obliged to consider seriously leaving his beloved
Uraniborg.

His choleric disposition, impatience and exacting nature had
here and there caused him trouble. Like most men of genius he
brushed everything but his work aside and, in a high-handed
manner, ignored accusations. This, however, could not be done
safely when dealing with the Crown and its officials.

The duties of a nobleman holding a fief were not onerous.
In times of peace he was required to perform the office of administrator, publish royal decrees, collect taxes, care for the forests and see that the property was kept up. Tycho took all these
responsibilities lightly, to say the least. Constant complaints
were made by his peasants of his cruel and unjust treatment of
them. All letters-patent conferring a fief upon a nobleman speci-
fied that the peasants thereon must not be abused by their lords.
As we have seen, King Frederik, after receiving the petitions of
the abused, had already sent Axel Gyldenstierne and Arild
Ugerup to Hveen to find out the truth of the matter. The findings had resulted in the king laying down the law as to what

could and what could not be rightfully demanded of the peasants by their irritable and obstinate lord. On top of this, only a
short while afterwards, a disagreeable process was brought
against Tycho by his Roskilde life-tenant, the farmer Rasmus
Pedersen, "whom he had put in irons and carried off from his
own table and taken to Hveen so that he no longer could return
to the farm he had rented from Tycho," and the case was decided against the lord of Hveen. When he appealed, the noblemen who acted as judges concurred in the earlier verdict. Such
rarely was the case in disputes between noblemen and their tenants, so the matter caused a bit of a stir and, to Tycho, considerable mortification.

A far more serious matter, however, was that of the Holy
Three Kings' Chapel at Roskilde. It was a long drawn-out affair that very naturally turned the young King Christian against
Tycho and did him no end of harm. The trouble had started
when the widow of the former canon, Henrik Holk, and also
the University of Copenhagen, complained that they had never
received any of the moneys which they were to have during the
"year of grace," following Holk's death. Holk had spent forty-
one years as canon so there was plenty of reason for the widow's
complaint. When questioned in the matter, Tycho simply paid
no attention to the letter written him.

Christian IV was unused to such arrogant and insubordinate
behavior on the part of any nobleman, let alone one who had
been shown many and large favors by the Crown. Tycho was
playing with fire, and the fact that he at various times in his
communications to his royal master emphasized that King Frederik had always been the protector of science probably did him
little good with his successor.

The Chapel of the Holy Three Kings at Roskilde, one of the
best-paying canonries, of which Tycho was the most favored
canon, had been built by Christian I, the founder of the Oldenburg line, and in it lay buried several of the kings of Denmark
including Christian IV's father and Tycho's benefactor, Fred-

erik II. In the short period during which the chapel had been in Tycho's care parts of the roof had been seriously damaged and permitted to fall in, risking the safety of the royal tombs beneath it. The king, informed of this, wrote Tycho and the chapter of the disgraceful state of affairs. Over a year went by, during which rain dripped on the royal sarcophagi, while Tycho, both because of absorption in his scientific work and from sheer forgetfulness, did nothing whatever. The king went personally to inspect the roofing, timberwork and vaulting, and for the sixth time wrote Tycho. Even this did not bring Tycho to his senses. Another year went by, whereupon came a final sharp reprimand reading:

"Receive our good graces.

"Know that we have previously written you that you should without negligence undertake the repairs of the Chapel in Roskilde Cathedral called the Holy Three Kings, in which are buried our forefathers of sainted and praiseworthy memory. This you have not done at all, so that said Chapel falls daily into greater disrepair and [is of] vexation [to us]. We are more than surprised that you have disregarded and paid no attention to our commands to repair this building. So we now order and desire you to give your entire attention to repair the aforesaid Chapel finally and without excuses by Christmas, at the latest, and in such manner as is requisite. If the repairs of the Chapel are not completed by the day and time mentioned, then we will command our representative in Roskilde to repair the Chapel at your expense, after which we will immediately give the fief with its properties and income to another. You are to inform us forthwith what you propose to do in the matter, so that we may know how to act. Such is our will. . . ."[5]

"Actum, Colding, Sept. 4, 1594."

Such a stiff reminder made Tycho see that His Majesty could no longer be trifled with, and that action was imperative. This

[5] The king always addressed everybody in the second person, "*Du*" ("thou"), except his councilors, whom he addressed as "*I*" ("ye").

he now finally took, but the harm was done, and King Christian quite naturally never forgot his negligence and disrespect in the matter.

The ill-feeling engendered against Tycho at court had further been added to by the Livmedicus (royal physician), Peder Severinus, whose ire as mentioned above had been aroused by many a fat fee lost from wealthy clients and foreign visitors who had received free medicines in Tycho's chemical laboratory. Less important *medici* might be laughed at, but not so the king's physician.

While these and other like unfortunate events were undermining Tycho's position, much had, on the other hand, been accomplished at Hveen. The exhaustive studies that Tycho had made of the comets he had observed in 1577, 1580, 1582 and 1585, and those of the eclipses of the moon in 1573 and 1580, became the basis of conclusions and writings that were to have far-reaching influence upon his science. He decided that comets were true celestial bodies, moving in fixed courses, rather than atmospheric phenomena as previously supposed, and by his tireless observations of the moon, he discovered its variations, the inequality in the inclination of its orbit and in the motion of its nodes, and determined laws governing the inequalities of the moon's motion. He noticed the influence of refraction and made allowance for it in calculating the altitude of the stars. He was later to prepare a table of refractions to $45°$, inferring that beyond that point refraction did not exist, an error which was, of course, the result of his imperfect instruments. Though his researches may have been imperfect, they represented an immense step forward. His discoveries as regards the lunar motion in latitude were as important as those he made of inequalities in longitude.

Ever since Tycho first began to study the heavens, the planets had been his favorite objects of research. Year upon year until his death he never neglected to take regular observations of them. And his work in determining the positions of the fixed stars continued with unabated, feverish excitement and interest. He felt the urgent necessity of a new accurate catalogue that would be built up on the basis of nine standard stars and twelve additional ones near the zodiac. The new catalogue when finally published comprised no less than 777 stars, all determined by the most laborious methods and all accurately placed on the Augsburg globe in his library. This in itself was a phenomenal accomplishment.

If one had asked Tycho what he felt was the most important work he had undertaken, he would probably have replied "My star catalogue," though we know now that it was dwarfed by the results of his observations of the moon and planets.

Such entries as he himself made in his Uraniborg diary are written in fine, strong, slanting strokes of the pen, reflecting the writer's vigorous character. No handwriting expert could study them without concluding that the writer was a person of force and determination.

Portions of his astronomical observations were written on the paper manufactured on Hveen and watermarked with a view of Uraniborg and the name "*Uraniburgum*." As the entries run along they give not only the daily weather report and the arrival and departure of guests and pupils, but also interesting historical events which are often inserted in the margins. The signs of the planets are frequently used to indicate the days of the week, as was the custom of the time, and signs are also used to indicate the sun and the moon. The weather must have been pretty bad on the island, for the days are generally described as "dark" or "nearly dark" or "stormy." Whenever a good one occurred, there is a joyous note in the entry: "Wonderful, clear weather all day long and rather quiet. Fine northwind!"

The entries in Danish in the diary have a certain amount of Latin interlarded, as was inevitable in everything a scientist or even a pseudo-scientist of the day wrote or annotated. Many entries are both so brief and so enigmatic in their abbreviations that one has to be pretty familiar with Tycho's life to puzzle them out. Thus Queen Sophia's visit on June 27, 1586, is referred to merely by: *"Reg,"* (Regina); Tycho's sister's marriage, some six weeks later by *"D. Soph. noct"*; his uncle Steen Bille's death by *"Sepultus Steno Bildt."* King James's visit, however, seemed worthier of a longer notice, for March 20, 1590, has the entry, *"venit mane H. 8, abiit H. 3.,"* and on April 19, 1590, when King James finally left Denmark to return to Scotland with his bride, occurs *"Rex Scotiæ circiter horam 7 P.M. Helsingora cum Regina sua et comitatu in regnum per mare discessit, Navali Regis nostri comitatus stipatus."*

Astronomical observations were recorded carefully in the diary, beginning with the year 1563, as were also observations of the comets that appeared in the years 1577, 1580, 1582, 1585, 1590, 1593 and 1596.

Another one of the daily tasks at Uraniborg was the keeping of the meteorological diary.[6] Tycho had commenced it in 1582, and it was continued until 1597, not a day passing without its entry, though neither thermometer nor barometer existed. Though the diary was kept by one or other of the more trusted assistants, principally Elias Olai Cimber (Morsing), Tycho would occasionally glance at it to see that the entries were to his satisfaction. The Gregorian calendar not having been as yet universally introduced into Protestant Denmark, the diary was kept in the old style.

In connection with the introduction of the new calendar, the following incident is mentioned by various of Tycho's biographers as having taken place during one of his Augsburg visits: The good citizens there had been notified out of a clear sky that the coming fourth of October (1582) was to be altered to the fifteenth, and every fourth year thereafter would have a day added to the month of February. One can readily understand the indignation of the Protestant Augsburg burghers and tradesmen that Rome should decree such an astonishing innovation

[6] Now in the Library of Vienna, written partly in German and partly in Danish script. The diary for the period 1582-1597 was published at Copenhagen in 1876 by the Royal Danish Society of Science and Letters.

and thus upset the entire business of the city. When Burgomaster Hainzel and the principal doctor of theology, Mylius, drove into the great market square, the populace showed that they would hear of no such nonsense. They pulled out their swords, seized the doctor, and locked him in the nearby baker shop. The guard had to be called to free him, and Hainzel called nobles, merchants and others to the city hall, while couriers were dispatched in various directions. Peace was finally restored.

Few besides Tycho and the more learned understood the reason for the Gregorian, reformed calendar. Scholars realized that any opposition on religious grounds was nonsense. It was a question of scientific accuracy and had nothing to do with theology. But, in Denmark, the mere fact that Rome had initiated the reform set the government against it and hindered the change from being adopted until as late as the year 1700.

In Tycho's printing establishment Weida was succeeded by a printer named Hans Gaschitz. The only book printed in Danish on Hveen, either by him or others, appeared in 1591.[7] It was a collection of about four hundred rules for foretelling changes in the weather by the appearance of the sky, the sun, the moon, the stars, and by the behavior of animals. Longomontanus wrote the introduction at Tycho's dictation and another pupil, Peder Jacobsen Flemløs from the island of Funen put the material together, some of it taken from Tycho's manuscripts and some from his observations. Its title, in English translation, was *An Elementary and Terrestrial Astronomy about Changes in the Weather.*[8]

Following are specimens of its advice: "Flies and fleas announce rain, when they are more than usually troublesome to men, horses and cattle. . . . When goats are so very greedy that you can neither by words nor blows hinder their biting off small shrubs, though they are not very hungry, then that is a sure

[7] Peder Jacobsen Flemløs, *En Elementish eller Jordisch Astrologia om Luftens Forendring.* Uraniborgi, 1591. See Bibliography.

[8] Longomontanus printed a new edition in 1644, at Copenhagen.

sign of rains or storm. . . . When pigs are throwing sheaves of corn or bundles of straw around with their snouts as if they were mad, you need not doubt there soon will be rain. . . . All kinds of unusual fire in the sky, looking like an army or like stars running to and fro or against each other, or falling down to earth, are forewarning of comets. . . . Earthquakes generally follow after great and long-appearing comets. . . . When the bees collect and carry small stones with their feet and legs in order to weight themselves down, then they fear that storm is shortly due."

The dedication stated that "Tyge Brahe has permitted this little book to be printed in the Uraniborg printing establishment, which he set up for the sake [of the printing] of his *Opera astronomica*, and as he now, for the same purpose, has paid for and prepared on Hveen a stock of paper for this same *Opera*, he did not wish that his printers should have a vacation and be idle, but has allowed them, for the time being, to take up this little work."

New pupils were constantly arriving at this period. Klaus Mule and David Fabricius came, while older ones left to enter the Church or medicine, or to engage in scientific pursuits elsewhere. Some were sent on errands, to present publications of the Hveen press to illustrious men or learned friends, to make purchases abroad or continue their studies there.

Over all these activities and the large, disorderly household Tycho ruled like a tsar on his seagirt little isle, constantly remedying some imperfection in his domain by this or that ingeniously contrived device. Difficulties were the breath of life to him: how to fashion an improvement in the sights of his instruments—for he knew well that the inevitable faults of even his best instruments must be taken into consideration—how best to drain a marsh or improve the fruit in his orchard, or rectify some other matter on the island. Impatient and positive, he supervised everything from morning until night. In his astonishing versatility and inventive, restless genius he might well be compared to the Italian giants of the Renaissance, Leonardo and Michelangelo. It was a thousand pities that the vexations of money and patronage could not have been kept far from his study and observatory.

There was no letting up on the hard daily and nightly work at Uraniborg, though Tycho complained about the constant stream of visitors who, naturally, broke in on his work. But when his sister Sofie arrived, she was always received with open arms, for she was rather a helpmate than a guest. Not so, however, when he was interrupted by the *Bär*, contemptuously referred to as the evil "Bear,"[9] with whom Tycho was to have so much trouble. Among frequent visitors were Holger Rosenkrantz, Axel Gyldenstierne and Bishop Jacob Madsen, Vejle, Gert Rantzau, the great Henrik's son and seneschal at Kronborg, Johannes Müller from Königsberg, called Regiomontanus, and Peder Munk, and a long list of others, great and small. They must often have been a nuisance disturbing the Uraniborg routine, and yet many of them were entertained in the great summer room or library, where the conversation would be both delightful and stimulating.

Little is known of Tycho's family life in these times; stars and planets were, as usual, the substance of his letters, though he often inquired about some baker or printer or skilled mechanic. In those days not only were such questions frequently asked but, if a lord was sufficiently powerful and the need imperative, he was not above sending his retainers to steal the man he wanted. Two boys were born to Tycho and Kirstine, Tyge in August 1581, named after his father, and Jørgen, about 1583, named after his uncle. When they were nine and ten years old the boys were sent to Sorø, the Eton of Denmark, which at that time accepted thirty sons of noblemen and thirty commoners. Owing to their mother's birth, the Brahes had to be enrolled among the latter.[10]

9 Nicolai Reymarus *Ursus* Dithmarsis (Nicolai Reymers Bär from Dithmarshen).
10 Both King Christian and his brother Ulrik had been among the noble scholars at Sorø where they were entitled by royal orders to ten courses for their dinner, "four of them decently cooked."

The work at Uraniborg was interrupted from time to time by trips to Copenhagen. Though Tycho was very matter-of-fact, believing little that could not be scientifically proved or actually experienced, his contemporaries recount that he refused to set out on a journey if on his way from Uraniborg to the dock, to board the boat that King Frederik had presented him with, he met either a hare or an old woman. Fortunately the road was a short one, and old women had seldom any business on the castle property. And then, we must remember, Tycho lived in a superstitious age and, however sensible, was bound to be influenced by its ways of thinking.

With his mechanical bent he installed at various points in Uraniborg contraptions and devices that were beyond the understanding of his servants or his peasants and naturally seemed like magic to them. He thus used to take pleasure in pressing a button hidden under his study table to signal, by its connecting cord and bell, to pupils in Stjerneborg to come to him. He whispered their names at the same time, telling the dumfounded onlookers when the pupils arrived that his voice had carried through all walls and over all space. And he had other devices that left them equally assured of his supernatural powers.

Books or minor instruments were the gifts Tycho usually received and valued the most. The one he prized above all others was a crude instrument that had belonged to Copernicus, consisting of frail pine staves and named by him his *Triquetrum*. The great astronomer had himself scratched the subdivisions on it in ink, and with it in his hands he had gazed at the stars. Knowing the value he would place upon this simple treasure, the cathedral chapter of Frauenberg had sent it by a pupil to the man they felt most worthy of receiving it as one following in the footsteps of Copernicus. On its receipt, Tycho's joy bubbled over, and, as was his wont on such occasions, he at once sat down and composed his thanks in Latin verse. He was, above all, very human and utterly unaffected.

Amid this Uraniborg bustle and business he had a loss

that affected him considerably. In his vast correspondence he appreciated the letters from Landgrave William of Hesse-Cassel more than those of anyone else. The landgrave had, time and again, proved himself a faithful friend; he was also no mean astronomer, so that their letters almost invariably concerned their science or something pertaining to it. Tycho had received no answer to his last letter or two to the landgrave, and the explanation finally arrived in the announcement of his friend's death. He wrote immediately to William's son, Prince Moritz, saying how much he hoped that the correspondence and the friendly relations with Hesse-Cassel might be continued in the next generation. He hoped also that he might have the prince's consent to carry out an idea he had for some time entertained, namely the publication of the more important of the landgrave's and his own astronomical letters, in order that others might benefit by the exchange of scientific views that had continued through so many years. With this request he enclosed an impassioned elegy.

The correspondence was published in 1596[11] under the title *Epistolarum astronomicarum, Liber primus.* The 176-page book was dedicated to Prince Moritz. In addition to the landgrave's and Tycho's letters—some in Latin and some in German, and all dealing with astronomical subjects—the volume also contained a number of letters from the landgrave's esteemed mathematician, Christopher Rothmann, and tables of longitudes and latitudes, observations on stars, comets and eclipses, descriptions and cuts of Hveen, Uraniborg, Stjerneborg, and their principal instruments. Finally there was a portrait of Tycho by the Augsburg painter Geyn. Under the portrait was written in Latin: "Here you see Tycho Brahe's picture; may the inner content [of the book], the hidden part, shine more beautifully!" On the back of the exquisite green leather binding was Tycho's coat-of-arms, surrounded by the

---

[11] Listed in Bibliography as *Epistolæ astronomicæ,* Uraniburgum 1596. Tycho intended to publish two more volumes of letters exchanged with scientists, but time was always lacking.

text: "Arms, family and property vanish, but a great mind, learning and nobility remain forever." The book was the work of both a fine printer and an artist. Whether because of the printing of this book or the usual constant shortage, the Hveen printer was in such need of paper that Tycho appealed to the king for help. As a consequence a royal letter was read at Ros-kilde, begging the good people to send Tycho Brahe their rags for his paper mill.

Despite difficulties, Tycho printed at the same time a small edition, which may be considered an annex to the *Epistolarum*, entitled *Icones instrumentorum qvorundam astronomiæ in-staurandæ gratia.*[12]

One can still find, here and there, beautifully embellished first editions of Tycho's publications, printed on his own Urani-borg presses, on his own paper, often covered with silk or velvet, still bearing witness to the skill of his artists and artisans. The refinement of the work testifies eloquently to their mastery of their craft.

Tycho's own collection of printed works produced in his shop remained in the family until necessity forced its sale. The books comprising ninety-seven works bound in forty-seven volumes were purchased by the Jesuits and are today in a special room in the Prague University Library. Some books belonging to Ty-cho's collection have been preserved elsewhere, in the libraries of Minichova (Bohemia), Gotha, Dresden, Vienna, Copen-hagen, Gothenburg, Brunswick, the Franklin Institute of Phila-delphia, and Bryn Athyn, Pennsylvania. All in all, 114 books are now known to exist bound in sixty volumes.

Luck was still with Tycho, for a decided windfall came to him at this time by the death in 1592 of Inger Oxe, Jørgen Brahe's widow, who had been like a mother to him and who now, as a last mark of her affection, left him quite a bit of her "ninety thousand daler worth of gold and silver-plate, bags of money and jewels." But it did not last long.

[12] This was a portion of the incomplete Volume I of *Astronomiæ instauratæ progymnasmata*, Volume II of which had been published in 1588.

CHAPTER EIGHT

The Lord . . . giveth . . . the ordinances of the moon and of the stars for a light by night.—JEREMIAH 31:35

CHAPTER EIGHT

NCE more the activities on Hveen were rudely disturbed by the arrival, by order of King Christian, of the two governors of Helsingborg and Landskrona, Christian Friis and Axel Brahe, to look into grave misdemeanors brought to the attention of the Crown either by jealous and malicious enemies or by wronged parishioners. The charges were so serious that Tycho's brother, Steen, who was a member of the Royal Council, was unable to help him. He was accused of having appropriated the fields of the Hveen parsonage, of having appointed and discharged in an illegal manner and without sufficient cause, one parson after another, of having torn down some of the parsonage's outhouses, of having omitted, for eighteen long years, to participate in the Holy Communion, of having led a deplorable life by sleeping with a concubine,[1] and finally of having never reprimanded, as was his bounden duty, the various parsons for omitting to exorcise the devil at baptism. Not wishing to be on hand when the peasants testified, particularly as one of the two judges was his brother, Tycho rashly absented himself for the occasion. The two governors listened to the complaints, investigated conscientiously and reported to the Crown. For the latter sin the incumbent parson was dishonorably discharged, while the lord of Hveen was instructed that his peasants were in the future merely to work for him two days a week from sunrise to sunset, to keep his dikes and fences in order, and to gather neither nuts nor wood without his special permission. If they failed in such duties, they were, however, merely to be punished by money fines paid to the landlord and a barrel of beer to the town folks. The entire controversy still further set the king against him, and very naturally so, for his conduct had again been reprehensible.

[1] *En Bislopperske*, or *Frillekone*, a contemptuous reference to his dubious marriage.

[137]

Tycho's new master may have been an exacting king, yet he was a great one and the first to be thoroughly Danish in thought and behavior. He wisely counterbalanced his hard drinking by hard exercise. In the words of one historian: "Monogamy never suited his exuberant nature, and the number of his bastards grew in time to be a Danish problem and a European joke. . . . As a king, Christian showed outstanding ability and courage, promoting the interests of his people both at home and abroad and combating the exorbitant claims of the nobility and encouraging overseas trade. If he did not altogether succeed, it was because he had to fight the rooted power of a selfish and irresponsible aristocracy at home, and abroad, the transcendent genius of Gustavus Adolphus. Throughout Christian's life too much always turned on the King himself; his intellectual powers and his character were always strained to their uttermost, for he had no deputies to lift the burden from him. His charm of manner, his masterful personality, his reckless courage, rough, astringent humor and moody temper had to be constantly at the service of his political acumen, and it was small wonder if the man was sometimes too tired to uphold the King unaided."[2]

King Christian had for some time been seriously embarrassed by lack of funds, badly needed for his attempts to build up his army and navy and to force Sweden to knuckle under to his wishes. To emphasize his financial distress he used as his motto the letters R. F. P.—*Riget fattes Penge*—"The Kingdom lacks money." The astute and resourceful Christofer Valkendorf urged that the only sensible way to obtain money rightfully belonging to the Crown was to make the nobles disgorge some of the fiefs which they had been so recklessly awarded. As Uraniborg and Stjerneborg were completed and the costly instruments purchased, he proposed that some of Tycho's financial benefits might well be withdrawn. If Tycho were hereafter merely to receive a portion of them, he would still be enjoying

[2] C. V. Wedgwood, *The Thirty Years' War.* New Haven, Yale Univ. Press, 1939, p. 204-205.

his master's bounty more than any other living scientist, it was argued.

Depriving Tycho first of his Nordfjord fief, which had yielded the considerable yearly income of a thousand daler, and then of Kullagaarden with its farms and the Kullen Lighthouse and the Sound revenues was, urged Valkendorf, in view of what had happened, a very simple matter. The king agreed, and as a consequence Tycho was stripped of first one and then another of his sources of income and a third of his benefices. Valkendorf has been accused of a long-smouldering dislike of Tycho, owing to the latter's refusal to give him one of his English mastiffs. He was, however, too big a man for such pettiness. For many years he had made out royal certificates for payments of large sums to the owner of Uraniborg.

Certainly this chancellor of the exchequer was not responsible for Tycho's next misfortune; the responsibility for that rested rather with the fortunate recipient of the favor involved, the high chancellor, Johan Friis. Tycho, however, considered both of them jointly responsible for his troubles. It is certain that Valkendorf, with an eye to the state coffers, could not constantly keep pouring out daler to the royal mathematician, particularly as Tycho's peasants were repeatedly complaining of his brutal treatment of them.

Staggering under the previous blows, Tycho was to his utter consternation, informed that he was also deprived of his fat Roskilde canonry. As such sinecures were generally given for life, he was bewildered to learn that it had been transferred to Friis, with its yearly revenues amounting to ten loads of corn and seven hundred daler. Friis already possessed another canonry, and Tycho therefore had good reason to feel more than aggrieved at this last deprivation.

Misfortunes never come singly. The sensitive and quick-tempered Tycho was now humiliated in his personal relations by two most disagreeable incidents. Among his various bêtes noires, none was worse than Nicolai Reymarus Ursus or (N.

Reymers Bär), generally referred to by Tycho as the "Dit-marsken Bear" or the "Plagarius." He had been a poor German boy who had first earned his keep as a swineherd, but by the time he was eighteen, mostly through his own efforts, he had learned Greek, Latin, French and mathematics. He became a tutor to young noblemen and entered the service of Erik Lange, the affianced of Tycho's sister, Sofie. He came to Hveen in Lange's train and, being already an able mathematician, challenged Tycho to a verbal encounter on this subject. Tycho's extreme vanity was outraged at being solicited to discuss such matters with a former swineherd. Tycho claimed that the "Bear" had grossly abused his stay as a pupil at Uraniborg, where he had spent part of his time correcting the proofs of the printing establishment, and had violated the hospitality and instruction given him there by "stealing in his *Fundamentum astronomicum* published at Strassburg in 1588, his master's system of the universe, a far greater treasure than any precious stone or bar of gold." Tycho also complained that he secretly made drawings of various Hveen instruments, and then after his departure pretended to the landgrave and other interested parties in the learned world that the ideas were his own. As soon as Tycho heard of the "Bear's" doings, he published violent letters against him in order to make known his robberies, though this gave little balm to his troubled spirit.

Most astronomers agree that Tycho's condemnation of Ursus was unfounded. The system that he claimed was "stolen" was one that would naturally have occurred to any student of astronomy who was not too blindly prejudiced in favor of either the Ptolemaic or Copernican theories. Indeed, Ursus was to go further than Tycho towards the Copernican theory in the matter of the earth's rotation. While Tycho insisted that the whole system whirled around the earth once every twenty-four hours, Ursus adopted the Copernican hypothesis of the rotation of the earth eastward once around its own axis every twenty-four hours.

The "Bear" rose to eminence and became professor of mathematics in Prague, whence he decamped when Tycho appeared on the scene. When Tycho finally threatened suit for the supposed theft, the "Bear" was dying of tuberculosis.

What, however, wounded the pride and haughty spirit of Tycho much more deeply than Ursus' supposed perfidy was the unfortunate betrothal of his daughter, Magdalene. For some years, two brothers, Gellius and David Joannes Sascerides, had been pupils at Uraniborg. They were sons of a Dutch immigrant from Alkmaar who had been professor of Hebrew at the University of Copenhagen. Gellius, after studying medicine, mathematics and astronomy, had taken advanced courses at Wittenberg and then came to Hveen, offering himself as an assistant. After a couple of years' work, Gellius obtained a royal scholarship with which he studied in Hessen, Basel and Italy, returning in 1593 to Uraniborg. During his six years with Tycho, the clever lad toadied himself by degrees into his master's good graces and, believing the match might assist him considerably on the upward path to worldly success, solicited the hand of Tycho's eldest daughter, Magdalene. She, as was usual in those days, was not consulted at all; but Tycho, liking the hard-working, brilliant assistant, and realizing the value of having him always beside him in his work, consented to the match.

However, in discussing the details of the wedding and settlement, the grasping pupil went too far in demanding a sizable dowry, whereupon Tycho lost his temper. He declared that he would not give both daughter and gold, and that Gellius should be more than happy and honored to marry a noblewoman, and should take her for her own sake. He further stated that he did not feel inclined to incur the heavy wedding expenses demanded, and that he expected Gellius to remain in his service for at least a year after the wedding. He also expected the groom to dress his wife as befitted a noblewoman.

The dispute growing increasingly acrimonious, Gellius left for Copenhagen and said nothing further about marrying. The ever-helpful and conciliatory sister, Sofie Brahe, next appeared and, after considerable diplomatic negotiating, believed she had patched up the trouble sufficiently to induce the lovers to step up to the altar. She wrote Tycho "that Dr. Gellius only wants a small, philosophical wedding with 'contract beer'[3] and says he will gladly promise, after the wedding, to stay at Hveen until next Easter." As Gellius did not put in an appearance, Tycho, considerably nettled, left for Copenhagen to have the matter settled one way or the other. Gossip was circulating throughout the capital, which naturally stung the Brahe pride. Tycho asked two of his friends, Krag and Bertelsen, "to corner the loose and wobbly character wherever he might be and ask him definitely: Did he or did he not want the girl?" When the worthy doctor was pressed, he replied that as far as he was concerned, Tycho Brahe could give his daughter to anyone he pleased. Upon hearing of this retort courteous Magdalene wrote to a friend: "How happy I am that the lad has so graciously freed and delivered me!"

Unfortunately, however, Tycho himself was far too infuriated to subside, especially as a betrothal in those days was considered as binding as a wedding. The berserker in him was aroused, and he decided to sue Gellius for breach of promise. In his complaint Tycho stated: "Gellius has falsely said that he did not know when and where the wedding was to be held, that his wedding clothes were not ready, that he had been expected to spend a year after the wedding at Hveen so as to learn more about the stars and his bride, all of which is nonsense. All I, Tycho, claimed, was that he should provide his bride with silk and damask clothes, and a statement that he would through life provide her with as good clothes as those in her wedding chest. And lastly, that I refused to give him a large sum of money which he demanded, I having answered that he could not have both gold and girl."

The university authorities were loath to have anything to do

[3] *Fæsteøl.*

with the case; nevertheless the suit very properly came up before the university senate, to which cases of manslaughter, wedlock and sorcery were usually referred. Both contestants had friends among the professors, who, in a similar case, had ruled that "it has always been the custom in this country that persons who are affianced and have testimony and proof of this and have given each other *Fæstendefæ*—such persons are wedded before God and man." All Copenhagen was agog, buzzing with excitement over the scandal. Tycho's enemies were of course delighted. In addition to the university authorities, others were called into consultation in so important and unusual a case. Crown councilors and the Bishop of Sjælland were sent for. After long discussion and many hearings *in camera*, the judges rendered a miserable verdict, neither accusing nor vindicating, but presenting what was termed "a contract of reconciliation" for the signature of both plaintiff and defendant.

Though this decision disgusted Tycho, it forced him to remain quiet for the time being. The matter had, however, embittered him to such a point that he opened up the *cause célèbre* once more a year or so later, and this time before the court of the cathedral chapter of Lund in Scania. Here the slippery Dr. Gellius Sascerides had succeeded in having himself appointed provincial *medicus*; and had even been given a promise of something better later.

In rehearsing the facts Gellius, when upbraided for having said that Tycho could give his daughter to anyone he pleased, was enough of a boor to reply that if he had so stated, "he must have said it either as a joke or because he was intoxicated."

The verdict on the appeal gave Tycho no greater satisfaction against his faithless son-in-law to be than that on the original complaint. Nothing came of it all, and Tycho received no restitution. The wicked flourished. Gellius married a rich woman, became professor of medicine at Copenhagen University, and remained an honored and important personage in the capital's learned circles, while Magdalene, who evidently had had enough of matrimonial ventures, lived and died a spinster.

The entire episode, however, played a considerable part in the critical decision Tycho now took to turn his back forever on Denmark. He had been deprived of his revenues, making continuation of his work at Hveen impossible. He was surrounded by enemies and had lost his king's friendship, and his good name was bandied about with ridicule and contempt. It is easy to understand what went on in his mind and heart.

In 1596 Christian IV had reached the age of nineteen, and the councilors decided to crown him. It was a most splendid and joyous occasion for both lord and beggar. Princes arrived from afar until every great house and inn was cram-jam full. Why, even the king had to borrow beds and bedding! It was Tycho's last great fete. He was in the midst of it and stayed for a fortnight of steady eating, drinking, fireworks, plays, tilting and general rejoicing.

There is no question but that Tycho loved his native land dearly, and his work on Hveen had been his life and joy. To decide to leave it all behind was the hardest task he had ever faced and all but broke his heart. He could not see that many of the difficulties that had arisen were due to his own errors and temperament. It was a pity that there was no one to take outside cares off his shoulders and attend with authority and conscientiousness to the thousand and one details pertaining to his large establishment, his numerous outside contacts and manifold activities. He should have had to concern himself only with his stars, his instruments, his printing presses and his friends.

Now that his fiefs and his prebend were gone, meaning a loss in his yearly revenue of some 2,400 daler, and merely the Hveen fief remained, it was out of the question to attempt to run the costly establishment of Uraniborg. Hoping against hope, Tycho made, however, a last half-hearted attempt to reclaim the position he had held by reminding the councilors of the letter he had received from them some years back. In this they had promised to do all in their power to perpetuate the astronomical observatory at Hveen, to encourage Christian IV as soon as he was of age to take steps to this end, and in the future to have the work continued by Tycho's descendants if they were fitted for it, or, if they were not, by other especially able noblemen or men eminent in the science of astronomy. The reminder was, however, to his final discouragement, pigeonholed without reply.

After deciding to leave Denmark, Tycho's first step was to sell his half of Knudstrup to his brother Jørgen. In doing so he especially stipulated that he reserved the right to continue to style himself "Brahe *til* Knudstrup."[4] In disposing of his half of the patrimony, Tycho may also have thought that at his death his sons, the offspring of a bondswoman, would probably be denied the right to any inheritance in the estate. His next step was to attempt to complete as far as possible some of the half-finished scientific work at Hveen, and to greet hospitably such friends as had been invited in happier days to visit him.

It is easy to imagine the bitterness in Tycho's soul. The whole world connected his name and exploits with Hveen, and now he was to be an outcast, a wanderer, and would have to attempt to start afresh, though he was old.[5] As often happens under such circumstances, lesser men commenced to snap contemptuously at his heels. Even Bishop Vindstrup of Lund started a religious persecution of him. In 1597 the last blow fell when King Christian deprived him of the stipend of five hundred daler accorded him by Frederik at the time that he received Hveen. The island fief itself could not be taken away, as its gift had been for life.

Heartbroken, Tycho finally brought himself to the great decision of leaving Uraniborg, and as a first step, he migrated to his Copenhagen house in Farvergade, which King Frederik

---

[4] The document bears the date of August 10, 1594, and is stamped with the seal of Eske Bilde.

[5] In those days a man of fifty considered himself old.

had formerly used for his city's dyeing establishment, but which was later granted to Tycho with the adjoining tower on the city walls. Two ignoramuses whom Valkendorf sent to report on what remained in Uraniborg after Tycho's departure reported that "the instruments, installations and the remainder of Tycho's work were costly and useless to anyone."

CHAPTER NINE

*And he brought him forth abroad,
and said, Look now toward heaven,
and tell the stars, if thou be able to
number them.*—GENESIS 15:5

Facsimile of Title Page of *Astronomiæ instauratæ mechanica*

Facsimile of Kepler's Entry in *Register of Observations* about Tycho's Illness

HEN Tycho left Denmark, he unquestionably expected and hoped some day to be urged to return. His departure was in a way inevitable, for he had come to be at odds with the three great powers of the day, the king, the Church and the nobility. Snapping one's fingers at the devil could not then be done with impunity.

After twenty-one years of restless, creative activity, Tycho and his wife, two sons and four daughters, his pupils and assistants, including his future son-in-law, Franz Ganzneb Tengnagel, and the able Longomontanus, some twenty in all, left Hveen forever on April 29, 1597. Books, presses, instruments and crucibles, everything was packed and shipped by boat to Copenhagen, except only the four largest, unmanageable instruments, which it was decided to leave in place until the definite haven of the wanderers had been determined.

The Copenhagen to which the saddened Tycho returned was no better and no worse than many of the middle-sized cities of his day. It was very dirty, not to say filthy, very unhealthy but most picturesque. Step-gabled buildings huddled around narrow thoroughfares, and lay scattered around the waterfront, a few of the more pretentious ones of brick, with tiled roofs, but most of them half-timbered, with tight and warm, but easily inflammable, thatched roofing. Above them all, and visible from afar in the flat countryside, rose the walls of the king's castle and the spires of St. Nicholas, the Holy Ghost's and Our Lady's Churches and that of the Blue Tower. The entire "King's Copenhagen," as it was and still is called, was crowded for yet a few decades inside its broad earthen ramparts.

Owing to the unsanitary conditions amid which the citizens lived, frequent plagues, particularly typhus, claimed large numbers of the population. During half a century no less than thirteen devastating plagues broke out. During the one that raged between 1550 and 1554 the University and schools closed and the court fled; other similar "warnings from God" arrived in 1568 and again in 1575 and 1585. Even the animals sickened. Comets appeared. It rained blood, and when one attempted to eat lamb, the flesh remained bloody after being well roasted. Property owners did not obey the city ordinances to keep the portion of the street facing their houses in tolerable repair; so when distinguished visitors were expected, the most dangerous holes were hurriedly filled with sand, preventing at least temporarily the breaking of horses' legs and the axles of vehicles. The slops and offal that were habitually emptied out of the windows were only partially eaten by the roaming swine, and the condition of the outhouses (known by the names of "Pilatus," the "House in Demand" or "The Secrecy") was indescribable. The churchyards were gathering places for pigs, dogs and cattle. Only three of the city wells were free from contamination, and a Copenhagen citizen of that time rarely used water for drinking purposes. The city officials were enjoined "above all to see that the children were given sufficient beer, so that they should not out of thirst take to water," and also "to see that all well-covers were securely locked, both in houses and yards, the moment water had been fetched, so that the children could not get at the wells and drink any water from them."

Everyone, rich and poor alike, ate and drank enormously. Beer and wine were the usual beverages, and aquavitae, a form of corn brandy, could be obtained from the apothecary. Gluttony and drunkenness were the order of the day. Unfortunately King Christian himself not only set a bad example among his cronies in his castle, but constantly had to be helped home after an evening's fun in the public inn, *Kompagnihuset*. One of the surgeon-barbers of the day published the following advice in the matter: "It is very good for persons to drink themselves intoxicated once a month, and for the excellent reasons that it frees their strength, furthers sound sleep, eases the passing of water, increases perspiration and stimulates their general well being." With such an admonition, no wonder there was no restraint. The remedy for the discomfort following a night's carouse was "a goodly portion of lard and hot cabbage," a meal that no doubt quickly relieved the victims of all they contained.

Brawls and murders leading either to the block or to the gallows—both affording public entertainment—were the material results of all the hard drinking. The streets and squares were in fact very dangerous places, and neither Tycho nor his apprentices, however peaceably inclined, ever ventured out in the evening without their rapiers. The worst offenders were the cabmen who collected in the city squares. They were constantly fighting. As their brawls repeatedly ended in murder, the king (who himself in a drinking bout had boxed his father-in-law's ears) complained to the chancellor, Peder Oxe, "that there is bad housekeeping here in Copenhagen, with one murder on top of another, and you do nothing about it."

Despite the lawlessness of Copenhagen, Tycho loved the city and his native Denmark and was loath to leave them. But there was still one last cup of bitterness for him to drain before he quitted his homeland. After he had reached the capital and was about to start his observations and chemical experiments there, he received orders forbidding him to do either. Persecution was following hard on the heels of injustice. Now that the dog was down, his enemies felt free to kick him. And it seemed to him that there was no use in his staying any longer; doing so merely meant prolonging the agony. He hired a boat sufficiently large to take his motley caravan and its belongings to Rostock, where he would find his trusted friends David Chytræus and Heinrich Brucæus. From there he hoped to explore future possibilities. Among these he knew he could first of all surely count upon his old, faithful friend, the great governor of Holstein, Henrik Rantzau.

Among his effects Tycho had a bag of money that represented

his half of Knudstrup. The Dukes Ulrich and Sigismund August of Mecklenburg, who were acting as regents during the minority of the Mecklenburg children, were in desperate need of funds. Tycho was thus able to negotiate a profitable loan of ten thousand of his "hard" Rigsdaler, in return for a note countersigned by ten of the duchy's wealthiest merchants as bondsmen, with the Doberau province in pawn as further security. Furnishing such a note was unusual, particularly when the principals were royal, but Tycho held to his demand until the dukes were forced to agree.

Homesick and desperate in his voluntary exile, Tycho foolishly decided while at Rostock to make a final attempt at reconciliation and so wrote King Christian a last letter giving an account of his unfortunate circumstances, as he saw them. To give greater effect to his plea, he begged Duke Ulrich also to write the young king on his behalf, and he made a similar plea to the elector of Brandenburg. The fact that he pulled every string he could think of indicates how pathetically anxious Tycho now was to retrace his steps, if possible.

Tycho's letter to the king was full of nostalgia and self-justification:

"Most puissant, noble King, my most gracious Lord, I most humbly present my willing and bounden duty. I most humbly beg to inform your Majesty, that whereas I had no opportunity of appearing before your Majesty prior to my departure, nor did I know whether so doing might be agreeable to your Majesty, I am now obliged briefly to inform your Majesty in writing what I would otherwise humbly have stated verbally:

"From my youth I have had a great inclination to study and understand thoroughly the praiseworthy science of astronomy, and to put it on a proper foundation, and for that purpose formerly hoped to remain in Germany in order to do so conveniently. Then your Majesty's father of blessed memory, when he learned of my intention, graciously desired and induced me to undertake and carry out my work at Hveen. This

I have done for more than twenty-one years with the greatest
diligence, and at great expense. I believe I have thereby shown
that I liked best to do it to the honor of my own Lord and
King of my country. And your Majesty's father graciously intended and promised that whatever I started in the said science
should be sufficiently endowed and perpetuated in an adequate
manner by a foundation. This your Majesty's Lady mother,
my most gracious Queen, undoubtedly still remembers and has
stated formally to the Privy Council of Denmark. In this matter I have received on parchment the resolution passed by the
Privy Council, confirming and further assuring me of this. Acting on this, I have taken much trouble and incurred great expense, even more than formerly, hoping that your Majesty,
upon assuming the Government, would be graciously pleased
to let me and mine profit thereby. But it has turned out differently from what I expected. In regard to this matter I will now
state only the following: Your Majesty is doubtless aware that
I have been deprived of what I should have had for the maintenance of the said science, and that I have been notified that
your Majesty does not intend further to support it, in addition
to which much else has happened to me (as I think) through
no fault or error of mine. By the grace of God, I hope to finish
what I have worked at so long and so earnestly, which is also
known to many foreign nations and greatly desired. I have not
myself the means to do this, as I have been so reduced that I,
notwithstanding the fiefs I held, have been obliged to part with
my hereditary estate. I thus trust your Majesty will understand
my necessities, and not be displeased with this my departure, as
I for these and other reasons greatly need to find other ways
and means so that what has been well begun may be properly
finished, and so that I may maintain my good name and reputation in foreign countries. But I have not departed with the intention of leaving forever my native land, but only in order to
look for help and assistance from other princes and potentates,
if possible, so that I may not be too much of a burden to your

Majesty and the Kingdom. If I should have a chance of continuing my work in Denmark, I would not refuse to do so. I should still, as formerly, much rather do as much as I could for the honor and praise of your Majesty and my own native land, in preference to that of any other potentates; that is, if my work could be done under favorable conditions, and without injury to myself. And if not, and it be ordained that I am to remain abroad, I shall always be subject to your Majesty with all respect and humility and in my humble capacity. I submit also for your Majesty's gracious consideration that it is by no means out of fickleness that I now leave my native land and relations and friends, particularly at my age, being more than fifty years old and burdened with a considerable household, which I, at great inconvenience, am obliged to take abroad. And all I have left behind me at Hveen proves that it has not been my purpose and intention to depart permanently thence. I hope, therefore, humbly, that when your Majesty considers these circumstances, your Majesty will be and continue my gracious Lord and King, and that I and mine may retain your Majesty's favor. I shall always remain humbly true and dutiful to your Majesty to the best of my ability, wherever the Almighty sends me. The same good God who rules all worthy governments grant your Majesty during your reign, happiness, blessing, good counsel and design."

This letter was dated from Rostock, the 10th of July, 1597.

Tycho could not have phrased a letter that would have done him more harm or hindered more conclusively any understanding that might ever have been reached between him and his sovereign. Christian, also a high-tempered man, was away in Germany when Tycho's letter arrived at Copenhagen Castle, but as soon as he returned and read it, he sent back a scathing reply, intended to put the unregenerate subject, once and for all, in his place. The king's missive was indeed quite unequivocal and left Tycho no alternative but exile:

"Christian the Fourth, by the Grace of God, of Denmark

and Norway, the Vends and the Goths, King, etc. Receive our favor as hitherto. Know that your letter which you have addressed to us from Rostock, the tenth day of last July, has been humbly delivered to us this week. In it you state among other things, first, that you had no opportunity to speak to us before you left this kingdom, nor knew whether it were convenient for us or not; and that therefore you have humbly wished to state your case in writing, and (you add) that we are doubtless aware that you have lost whatever support you hitherto have had for the maintenance of the science of astronomy, that we will not continue the support of this science, and that other things have unexpectedly occurred and happened to you through no fault or error of yours, as *you* think. Furthermore, you state that you have not yourself the means to support the science through your own means, and that even when you possessed your former fiefs you became so impoverished that you were obliged to part with your estate. And despite the fact that you, for these said reasons, are obliged to seek in other places from foreign potentates and lords, help, assistance and counsel in order to prosecute the science of astronomy, you beg us not to regard your journey with displeasure, particularly as you do not intend definitely and irrevocably to leave your native land. Further, you state if you were permitted to continue your work in this kingdom, you would not refuse to do so, but grant us this honor, on condition that your work could be undertaken under favorable terms and without injury to you—all as detailed in your lengthy letter.

"Now we would graciously have you consider: first in regard to your having had no opportunity to speak to us before you left the kingdom, inasmuch as you did not know whether doing so would please us or not: You well remember that you stayed in this City of Copenhagen for some weeks before you left the kingdom, and not only did not ask our permission to leave the country, as you should have done, but never even spoke to us except on one occasion when the peasants of Hveen and you appeared in Court before us and you were commanded and ordered to appear before us at the castle. Although you do not blush to make your excuses for this as if you were our equal, we desire to let you know in this letter that we are aware of all that has happened and that we expect from this day forth to be respected by you in a different manner, if you wish to find in us a gracious lord and king. As regards your not doubting that we are aware that you have lost some fiefs which you held, and your believing this happened owing to no fault or error of yours: You remember well what complaints our poor subjects and peasants of Hveen have brought against you, your behavior in regard to the church there, from which you for some years took the income and tithes and appointed no churchwarden, letting the church fall into ruin. You also remember that you took the land belonging to the parsonage and partly pulled down its houses. And as for the parson, who should live there and use the land for the keep of himself and his wife, you gave him a few pennies weekly and fed him in the company of your laborers. During a series of years, moreover, there was one parson after another, who had received no call from the congregation in accordance with the law, nor was lawfully dispossessed. Everybody is well acquainted with the manner in which the baptismal rite was omitted for a long time and with your cognisance. All of which, as well as other things which have occurred on that poor and small territory, and which were known to us long before the public knew of them, have caused us to grant our tenants and the Crown's fief to others who would administer them according to the law, justice and established customs.[1] With regard to your not being sufficiently wealthy to promote the science of astronomy through your own means, and your being obliged to leave the kingdom so as to ask for help of foreign potentates, but without the intention of leaving your native land altogether, and your begging us humbly not to take umbrage at your journey: There is great doubt whether you have spent on

---

[1] The king refers to the Nordfjord fief and Roskilde canonry. Since Tycho had received Hveen for life, he could not be deprived of that.

astronomical instruments the moneys you received for the property you sold, as it is rumored here that you have lent the
moneys, in thousands of daler, to lords and princes, for the
benefit of your children, and thus not for the honor of the
kingdom or the promotion of science. It is also very displeasing
to us to learn that you seek help from other princes, as if we or
our kingdom were so poor that we could not afford it, and you
were forced to leave with your wife and children to beg for help.
But whereas this has now been done, we have to leave it so, and
do not trouble ourselves as to whether you leave the country or
stay in it. Lastly, as you humbly state that if you were permitted
to finish your work in this kingdom you would not refuse to do
so, if it could be done without injury to you. Now we will graciously answer you that if you wish to serve as a mathematician
and do as you are told, then you should begin by first offering
your services and by asking about them as a servant should,
rather than saying in such emphatic words [that you would not
refuse to be reinstated]. When that is done, we shall know how
to state our will. And whereas your letter is somewhat peculiarly
expressed, and full of audacity and lacking in sense, just as if
we were obliged to render you an account of the reason we made
any change in the Crown estates, and whereas we remember how
you published in your epistles various nonsense about our dear
father, to the injury of his love for you and merely to relieve
your feelings, so we now forbid you by this letter to publish the
letter you wrote us, unless you wish to be punished properly by
us. We commend you to God. Written at our Castle of Copenhagen, the 8th of October, *anno* 1597.
"Under our Seal.

CHRISTIAN

"To our beloved, honorable and noble Tyge Brahe of Knudstrup, our man and servant."

Despite his letter to King Christian and those his royal friends
had written upon his solicitations, Tycho could not have had

much hope of a reconciliation with the king. In any case, as soon as the plague broke out in Rostock he accepted his friend Henrik Rantzau's offer of, temporarily at least, settling down at Rantzau's castle of Wandsbeck[2] just outside Hamburg. From there Tycho intended to sound out such potentates as might be most likely to engage and support, in a worthy and adequate manner, Europe's greatest astronomer.

Henrik Rantzau, governor of Holstein, was one of the great men of his day in Northern Europe, and a scion of the fine warrior, Johan Rantzau from Holstein, who at the head of his mercenaries had conquered the Duchies of Slesvig and Holstein for Denmark under Christian III. Henrik had been sent as a boy to Wittenberg, where he found rooms in Martin Luther's house, and often ate at his table. A few years later, while living with the Duke of Holstein in Brussels, he served as a page in the household of Charles V. He was in every way a magnificent character, playing an important role in Holstein where he served successively three Danish kings. He ruled well and economically and was constantly consulted by Frederik II. After this king's death he had a violent disagreement with Queen Sophia, who attempted to take over the regency of the province, but even this difficulty his diplomatic skill surmounted. In addition to his own wealth he acquired through marriage to a rich Brunswick heiress no less than eighteen castles. An astute business man, he loaned his gold at most advantageous rates to Charles V, as well as to other crowned heads and some of the great free cities. He was exceedingly intelligent and highly educated, deeply interested in the literary and artistic life of his time, and he had published two widely read books on astrology. In the Low Countries he had come into close contact with the glories of the Renaissance and the free breath of humanism, and had earned the title of "The Learned." One of his aims was to introduce into his country, Denmark, much of what he had

[2] Also called Wandesborg, and Wandesburgum.

learned and seen abroad and to make of his own home a Medicean center of culture. He was proud of his elegant Latin epistolary compositions, he was proud of the more than six thousand carefully selected volumes in his library, he was proud of his twenty-four grandchildren, he was proud of his astronomical and astrological knowledge and finally he was proud of his learned, scientific friends.

Tycho was received with open arms by this splendid governor, for he was exactly the type of man Henrik Rantzau delighted to honor, and was, moreover, an old friend and correspondent who had often welcomed Rantzau's son at Hveen. No more suitable place could possibly have been found for Tycho's work than the newly erected castle at Wandsbeck, now placed in so princely a manner at the disposal of Tycho's motley entourage, who were to remain there for two years. Here was every facility for astronomical work, even an admirably constructed observatory at the top of the building.

Since Henrik Rantzau was almost as ardent an astronomer as Tycho, it is interesting to note certain of his stellar observations. He writes: "The fall of man and the influence of the stars are what cause sickness. God has created the stars not only so as to enable us to calculate the years and months and days, but also so as to enable us, by observing their positions, to draw conclusions as to the future. The lower [organisms] depend upon the higher. The celestial bodies have a certain secret influence and effect upon bodies here below, and the liquids contained in our bodies are altered and increased or diminished according to the position and character of stars or planets. The moon in particular influences the liquids; when it is increasing in size, the liquids and blood and marrow of both human beings and animals likewise increase." Tycho agreed with Rantzau that the moon influenced the liquids in the body and that the brain, blood and marrow all increase or decrease according to the moon's position. Medical science of the day followed Tycho's belief and acted upon it in purging and bloodletting—even in considering the right time for hair cutting.

Upon his arrival Tycho opened his heart to his host, confided to him his most secret formulas for the treatment of various diseases, and told him of his hopes of finding patronage in high places. While his assistants and pupils were installing instruments, records and printing presses, Tycho set the wheels in motion in all possible quarters. The most likely prospect was the Emperor Rudolph II in Prague. Tycho's good, influential friend there, the former vice-chancellor Jacob Curtius, had unfortunately died, but his successor Caraducius and the influential chief physician, Thaddæus Hagecius, were both as well disposed towards Tycho as Curtius had been. Tycho wrote them at once, expressing his eagerness to enter the emperor's service. Rantzau wrote to the elector of Cologne, begging him to put in a good word for Tycho with Rudolph, and Tycho also appealed to the margrave of Brandenburg, who happened to pass through, rather the worse for wear after attending the wedding of his daughter. As a result the margrave wrote both his daughter and his son-in-law, "as soon as his head had been comforted with wine," pleading Tycho's cause. So as to leave no stone unturned, Tycho sent Tengnagel to Holland, with a copy of his new book under his arm, to see what his friend the Leyden professor, Joseph Scaliger, might be able to effect with Prince Moritz of Orange or the Grand Pensionery, Olden-Barneveld.

Feeling that possibly the best way to press his suit with the emperor might be to send him a description of Hveen with illustrations of all his magnificent instruments, together with an autobiographical account of his career and a list of his discoveries, for which much of the material, including woodcuts, was on hand, he set the printing presses in motion. A skillful printer, Philip von Ohr, was engaged in Hamburg, and under the heading *Astronomiæ instauratæ mechanica*, Tycho published a book

of 42 pages in elegant folio form, at the end of the year 1598.[3]
It was, naturally, dedicated to the emperor:

Ad Augustissimum Imperatorem
Rudolphum Secundum

Only a few presentation copies were printed.[4] Seventeen of the
principal instruments were reproduced, including the famous
Uraniborg wall-quadrant and the great Augsburg globe. Opposite each instrument was a detailed explanation of its use. Then
there was a portrait of Tycho at the age of fifty-two, a map of
Hveen, dissertations on the sun, the moon, the planets and the
fixed stars, copies of letters exchanged with Curtius and Patavinus, a Latin poem by Holger Rosenkrantz, and illustrated
descriptions of Uraniborg and Stjerneborg. Each page was
richly embellished with colored vignettes, ornamented capital
letters and cartouches. It was in fact the very finest work Tycho
and his printer could turn out, and it should, he hoped, prove a
successful introduction to Rudolph. Each richly bound copy
sent out, besides that for the emperor, had an appropriate personal dedication.

So as to impress Rudolph still further, Tycho had his pupils
copy in red and black lettering a few lists of the thousand
stars, the positions of most of which his long years of labor had
now definitely determined.[5] These lists were intended to replace the faulty Ptolemaic ones. The catalogue had been built
up on the basis of nine stars and twelve additional stars near
the zodiac. In determining a star, Tycho had measured the
declination directly by his armilla or a meridian quadrant, and
the distance from a known star, with a sextant.

[3] The book was reprinted in Nuremberg four years later and, on the three-
hundredth anniversary of Tycho's death, the Swedish Academy of Science published a reprint of the original. The whereabouts of fourteen copies of the original
folio are now known. See also Bibliography.

[4] Two copies, the ones sent Christian IV and the Archbishop of Lübeck, are in
the Royal Library in Copenhagen, one bound in green velvet, the other in a mauve
brocade. Tycho's arms and portrait are stamped on the outside. Christian's copy is
printed on parchment.

[5] While Tycho had made good observations of 777 stars, he filled up the list of
1,000 with hurried, preliminary observations of the balance.

[161]

It is to be noted that most of Tycho's observations, made in order to determine accurately the positions of the fixed stars, had been undertaken before the end of 1592 and had been embodied in his catalogue of the 777 printed in the *Progymnasmata*. Observations of Mars, Jupiter and Saturn were his principal concern between 1593 and 1595, at which date he once more resumed his work on the fixed stars, continuing this until 1600, in order to bring their number up to one thousand.

Tycho's oldest son, Tyge, was dispatched with the two treasures from Wandsbeck to Prague, while other messengers scurried around Europe with those intended for the Archduke Mathias, the Vice-Chancellor Caraducius, the Archbishop Wolfgang Theodor of Salzburg, the Bishop of Lübeck, Professor Brucæus in Rostock, the Hainzel brothers in Augsburg, Prince Moritz in Cassel, son of the deceased Landgrave William, the Prince of Orange in Amsterdam and Scaliger in Leyden.

During his Wandsbeck stay, Tycho felt the full impact of what had happened, and a depression seized him that was unusual to his buoyant nature. In his violent uprooting, the mother-earth had come with him, but provided him, so it seemed for the moment, little from which to draw inspiration. Something was constantly gnawing at his vitals—homesickness, injured pride, humiliation, loneliness. He had paid a heavy toll for his lack of prudence and foresight. The two sides of his nature fought within him, one cold and intellectually calculating, the other emotional to overflowing. Had the years of hard, meticulous labor brought him anything but old age, banishment and disgrace? He might have lacked worldly prudence and foresight, but how lightly they weighed in the scale against what had been his aim. Had he not unraveled the laws of heaven, and by his accuracy come nearer to the truth than any of his predecessors? It had never occurred to them, not even to the great Copernicus, to verify the stellar positions handed down from antiquity. Though his observations had not absolutely proved the harmony that must be there, they had come very close to it. Had anyone employed instruments similar to those his ingenuity had invented, or surpassed them in splendor of construction? He had been accused of being overbearing and arrogant, intolerant and contemptuous of the ignorant. But had he not been pestered by trivialities when he wished to remain undisturbed to prosecute his work? And had he not despised the shams of life with which he was surrounded?

On two great questions he had placed himself in opposition to what that great thinker Aristotle had taught, and yet he was right in both: the star in Cassiopeia *was* a true fixed star, and the comets were no atmospheric phenomena, but *were* real heavenly bodies.

Rosenkrantz, Rude, Bille, Ulfstand, Trolle, Gyldenstierne, Rosenspar—all his contemporaries had reached high and honorable positions, and here was he groveling to the mighty all over Europe in order to be able to continue his work!

Such bitter thoughts and remonstrances crowded helterskelter through his usually orderly mind, while he paced the Wandsbeck terrace or sat for the first time in his life, indolent and unobservant before the starlit heavens, almost breaking under the burden of the manifold contradictions of his nature—his wild emotions and his shrewd powers of judgment and self-criticism. Attempting to shake himself free, he reached for one of his large sheets of paper and composed his lament to Denmark, filled with longing and complaint. He began:

> What have I done, O my homeland, since
>   now you so coldly reject me,
> I who have raised your name to honor and
>   greatness eternal?
> Can you with anger contemplate the industry
>   I have expended?
> Which of your children have given as freely
>   of gifts as my portion?

In the days of the future my labor will surely
redound to my credit.[6]

He printed its Latin verses and sent them to a few chosen
friends.

It was told that King Christian in visiting Wandsbeck after
Tycho's departure passed an open book in which Tycho had
copied the verses. The king stopped, read them through atten-
tively, and then passed on deep in thought, oblivious of his host
and courtiers.

Henrik Rantzau, conscious of his friend's despair and fully
appreciating what an original thinker and independent spirit he
was, did his utmost to distract and interest him and to make
him return to his usual pursuits in which he was, for the time,
ably assisted by Johannes Müller (Regiomontanus), the elector
of Brandenburg's mathematician.

The productions of his printing press were naturally a great
distraction, as was also his correspondence, which continued unabated. He wrote to the all-powerful Valkendorf, hoping to
receive a last bit of income from the lost Nordfjord fief and
arrears and dues from his Hveen tenants. "If it were known,"
he said, "how contrary and disobedient the peasants on that little
island were, and what I suffered from them all the time I lived
there, all the while not losing patience with them, and being
much kinder than they deserved, then perhaps people would
think differently about them than they have done."

The poor fellow had learned nothing. He wrote to his
brother Steen, and also to Holger Rosenkrantz, who had married his niece, both of whom had stood by him in his troubles
and understood that he had been his own worst enemy, telling
them of the upheaval in his life and his hopes for the future.
He repeated the same story in his letters to the best of his scien-

[6]ELEGIA AD DANIAM

Dania, quid meruo? Quo te, mea Patria, læsi, ·
Usque adeo, ut rebus sis minus, æquæ meis?
Scilicet illud erat, tibi quo nocuisse reprendar,
Quo majus per me nomen in orbe geras?
Die, age, quis pro te tot tantaque fecerat ante,
Ut veheret famam cuncta per astra tuam?

Tycho Brahe's Tombstone

The Teyn Church in Prague

Excavation of Stjerneborg 1901

Ruins of Uraniborg 1846

tific friends throughout Europe. The child in him is shown by
the fact that, despite all, he still clung to the possibility of re-
tracing his steps.

In the second year of his stay at Wandsbeck, the long-
awaited imperial couriers arrived with letters from Caraducius
and Hagecius. They wrote that the Emperor Rudolph would
be happy to receive Tycho with every mark of favor and generosity! The emperor sent word that if what he had decided
to give him did not suffice, his hand was not closed, "nor
need Tycho's mouth be glued." The first emotion and excitement in the castle having subsided, Tycho decided to
depart at once, accompanied by sons, pupils and instruments,
but for the time being, and until proper quarters had been allo-
cated by the emperor, to leave his womenfolk behind him. He
thanked Rantzau for his hospitality, packed his belongings and
started off. On reaching Dresden Tycho received to his dismay an
alarming letter from Caraducius telling him that the plague was
raging in Prague, that the emperor and his court had left for
Pilsen, and that he did not wish him to arrive until it was once
more safe to live in the capital. Tycho's old favorite haunt of
Wittenberg being so close by, to the northwest on the Elbe, he
decided to take his caravan there for the winter, or at least until
he received word that it was safe to proceed. To his joy, he
found lodgings in Melanchthon's old house, where former
friends and scholars, and particularly Professor Johannes Jessen
(Joannis Jessenius) welcomed him even more cordially owing
to his misfortune and altered circumstances. Tycho and his sons
enrolled themselves as students at the University. The only fly
in the ointment was the rekindling of his old dispute with Ursus
("the Bear"), who had become professor of mathematics at the
famous old University of Prague. Acrimonious notes passed
back and forth between them, Tycho calling his enemy "half-
cracked" and vowing that when he reached Prague he would get
even with him. Fortunately, shortly after Easter 1599, word arrived that the danger was over in Prague and that the emperor
was ready to receive the great Danish astronomer.

[165]

CHAPTER TEN

There is one glory of the sun, and another glory of the moon, and another glory of the stars: for one star differeth from another star in glory.—

I CORINTHIANS 15:41

UDOLPH II, the grandson of Charles V and son of Maximilian II, had a strange personality. He took no interest in ruling or in political matters of his empire or his kingdom. Listless and devoid of energy in matters of state, he spent hours speculating upon natural history, astronomy, astrology and chemistry, or in admiring his extraordinary collections of antique and modern art objects, the greatest of his age. He had been brought up in Spain and at an early age had learned various of the languages of his far-flung possessions. He was both clever and cultivated and something of a scholar and an artist. Nothing pleased him more than to surround himself with learned men and enter into interminable discussions with them. That to him was a far more pleasant occupation than harassing his mind with the constantly troublesome Hungarians and Turks. By dint of hard work he had succeeded in making Prague the center of European spiritual life, though the Spanish Jesuits had done their best to hinder him in this. He did so much to revivify the University of Prague, the oldest in the German Empire, founded in 1348, that it had become the empire's leading institution of higher learning. Some thought Rudolph melancholy and constantly suspicious, unbalanced at times to the point of being out of his head. But then what did most people really know of the secluded and unapproachable ruler?

The emperor's scientific predilections being what they were, Hagecius had encountered little difficulty in urging the employment of the famous Danish astronomer. Upon the arrival of Tycho's party they were received with proper honors by the imperial councilor, Barvetius (Barwitz). He escorted them to Tycho's dear old friend Curtius's magnificent home, still occupied by his widow, but offered to Tycho as lodgings until the proper place for his work had been discussed with the emperor himself.

Having dressed himself in his best feathered cap and doublet and put the books he was to present to the emperor under his arm, Tycho proceeded the following morning to the nearby Hradschin Palace to be received in audience. Tycho described what passed between him and Rudolph in a letter he wrote home to Vedel, observing that to his pleasure the conversation had been conducted entirely in Latin rather than in German.[1]

"We talked about my annual salary, which I left for the Emperor himself to decide; he then granted me an assured income of 3,000 gulden,[2] in addition to various undetermined 'accidents,' which amounted to an additional thousand. Some of the Council had been against this, stating that there was no one at court, not even among the counts and barons, who had been in the service for a long while, who received as much as this annually.

"But as the Emperor had insisted that such would be the case, and as neither the Master of the Court, Herr Rumphæus, nor the Chief Marshal, Herr Traubson, nor any of the most important dignitaries, advised against it, it was decided to pay me at once 2,000 gulden as a mark of honor. Yes, the Emperor even allowed that my salary was to date back to the time I was first appointed, though I had only just arrived, and had not wished earlier to acknowledge any other Lord [than King Christian]. The Emperor, in addition, promised me, out of his own free will, a fief to be inherited by my children, as soon as a fief was vacant in his dominion, so that my family would be cared for after my decease."

Wishing at once to avail himself of Tycho's insight into future events, the emperor had improved the occasion by questioning him as to the wisdom of his taking a bride. Tycho replied that if he did so, any son born to them would be tyrannical,

---

[1] The learned fraternity of those days not only constantly interlarded their speech and letters with Latin phrases, but wrote their letters so frequently in Latin that we find one of the professors of Copenhagen University apologizing for not using Latin in a letter to the faculty, and expressing his hope that he had not thereby vexed his colleagues.

[2] The gulden had about the same value as the Danish daler.

cruel and barbaric. The wisdom of the advice was proven in an ironic way when his mistress had a son; he exhibited, when grown, the characteristics prophesied by Tycho.

Tycho left the imperial castle on the crest of the wave. Everything he had dared hope for in his strange new life had at last come true. But Prague had its defects. In addition to being a disturbing, noisy place, it must have been very foul and dirty. A contemporary English traveler observes: "Except the stench of the streetes driue backe the Turks or they meet them in open field, there is small hope in the fortifications thereof." The Curtius house was ill-fitted for observation and the setting-up of instruments. Furthermore, Tycho did not wish his old friend's widow to be dispossessed of her home, and so he broached discreetly the subject of another domicile. What was passing through his mind is shown by his writing. "The astronomer must be cosmopolitan, for every country is a fatherland of the mind. But all places are not fitted for the astronomer's work; for this he needs specially equipped buildings, with free horizons on all sides, away from the noise of the world, and philosophical peace for his studies."

Hearing of his difficulties, the emperor informed Tycho he might have the choice of any one of three castles in the environs of Prague, which he would gladly order fitted up for his work. Tycho himself was to choose which might prove most fitting *"zur Exercierung seines Studii."* Tycho selected the castle of Benatky,[3] recently purchased by the emperor from Count Dona. Concerning it he wrote his friend Erik Lange: "It is situated on a height, so that one has a free horizon on all sides. It has splendid and comfortable buildings. Close by lies a small town, on the river Isar, which is a tributary to the Elbe. It is five miles from Prague, with a road by which you can reach it in six[4] hours. Here I have, God willing, decided to settle with my family, until I am given a fief in some other place, which the Emperor

---

[3] Also written "Benach" and "Benatck."

[4] Tycho was of course figuring by the Danish mile, which equals four English miles.

has promised me and my successors. In the meantime the Emperor will give me a comfortable house in Prague, which I can enjoy as often as I go there."

And again he wrote: "Everything at home was disagreeable, everything had to be paid for by me, while here the Emperor does it all willingly. I thank God that I have been freed from all the hardship which I, though innocent, have borne so long and patiently. . . . Here all great and noble persons favor and love me." A little later he wrote again: "Thank God everything seems to be turning out right, and I hope it may soon be even better, so that I, by God's grace and foresight, will in no way regret that I and mine have left Denmark. I only wish we had done so long ago."

The Bohemian start had thus been a most happy one—up to now everything had been *couleur de rose*. Obtaining speedy payment of the promised money proved, however, a most difficult undertaking. The court referred the matter to the bursar's office, then to the Silesian and Bohemian exchequers, which shuttled Tycho's requests back and forth.

Captain Kaspar von Mühlstein was in charge of the castle of Benatky and the district in which it lay. He was now to be in charge of the multifarious alterations and the large expenditures ordered right and left by its new occupant. Mühlstein, whose previous existence had been quiet and orderly, soon felt that he would go mad before the work was completed and the Dane settled and satisfied.

Judging from the emperor's gracious condescension towards him in other matters, Tycho concluded that he might order pretty much anything done to the sadly run-down Benatky that his extravagant and demanding fancy might suggest. As a result he instructed the frantic Mühlstein to build an observatory on top of the castle and a chemical laboratory with many ovens at its bottom. He ordered walls razed, windows ripped out, extensions thrown out, terraces extended—in fact, he turned the edifice inside out and upside down. Wood was to be cut from the forest and charcoal burned for the ovens.

The captain countered by saying that Tycho could not give such orders or authorize expenditures on such a scale without the sanction, in each instance, of the exchequer. Any order, he continued, would in turn have to be countersigned by the imperial councilors, and in this case, where it entailed the metamorphosis of a Crown estate, the emperor himself would have to signify his august approval. To all of this Tycho replied that he would inform the councilor Barvetius of his difficulties and maltreatment and thus cut the matter short, for surely the emperor wished him to have what was required for the prosecution of his work. In the end, Tycho, by dint of perseverance, obtained everything he desired—whether there was cash in the imperial strong-box or not—including a thousand dalers yearly from the receipts of the property. The vineyards and orchards stretching down to the river at Benatky looked up at such activity as had not been seen for centuries.

The alterations being well advanced, Tycho next concerned himself with the furnishings. Tengnagel and Fabricius were sent off to Wittenberg to bring the womenfolk on, for, as there was plenty of work for them, their presence became highly desirable. Tycho's son, Tyge, his assistant Longomontanus and his pupil Mulæus (Klaus Mule), were sent to Hveen to assist in packing and bringing on what was of far greater concern than the women of the family, namely, the four large instruments that had been left behind at Tycho's departure. To assist them in this, he wrote to ask his influential Danish friends to do their best to help. The ladies arrived, but not the instruments. It was a long way for huge crates to travel by cart or boat. The councilors wrote; even Rudolph was forced to assist by writing the senates of the cities of Hamburg and Magdeburg to expedite their arrival. The severe winter and the freezing of the Elbe, as well as the hostility of these free, proud cities, independent toward the Austrian government ever since the formation of the

Schmalkaldian League, caused further delays. At long last, however, the instruments also arrived, having traveled by Lübeck, Magdeburg, and up the Elbe to Leitmeritz, and with them came a quantity of salt fish sent as a last souvenir from Hveen.

A certain amount of order having replaced the earlier Benatky chaos, Tycho considered his working force and the proper allocation of their duties. Feeling the need for a partner in his labors, he had for some time had his eye on Johann Kepler, a young man only twenty-eight years old; Tycho was at that time fifty-two. He admired wholeheartedly Kepler's book, *Prodromus*, and he had the intellectual generosity to acknowledge that, despite their difference of opinion on the planetary system, the younger scientist was, to judge from his writings and correspondence, one of the most brilliant scholars of Europe.

For the first time in his life Tycho realized that he needed beside him someone considerably superior to an assistant. Despite the unabated prosecution of his astronomical work and the repeated favors and friendly protection shown him by Emperor Rudolph, homesickness, hidden deep, and not even acknowledged to himself, was constantly gnawing at his heart, depressing and laming him. Moneys promised him in Denmark had always been promptly paid, but there were interminable difficulties and delays in obtaining the expected Bohemian payments. He had been master of all he surveyed on his small island; that was far from the case now. Had King Christian offered him an opportunity to return, there is little doubt that he would have jumped at the chance. Tycho was no longer his old buoyant, enthusiastic self. He was a stranger in a foreign land, and everything in him yearned for his tiny seagirt dominion, where he had spent over twenty of the richest, most resourceful years of his life. He longed for Denmark, for Hveen, even for its comforting, enveloping fogs, at times so thick you could almost hear them move. His longing carried him back to Uraniborg, where he had watched the slow laying of every blessed course of its bricks and supervised the carving of every stone ornament. It was his creation as truly as his children were of his flesh and blood, and could never truly belong to anyone else. He needed the salt tang of the sea air, the crunch of the sand under his feet, and the busy stir about his gardens and bindery and presses. Tycho's proud spirit was breaking as memories crowded thick upon him. He was not well at all, a fact that added further to his mental dejection.

If his departure from Denmark had been his greatest misfortune, his meeting with the future creator of theoretic astronomy, whose laws were to make the planetary system clear, was ample compensation for the hardships of his exile. At the moment Johann Kepler was in a difficult situation. His position as a university professor of mathematics, astronomy, history and ethics at Graz, and mathematician to the Province of Styria, was in danger. His very presence in the country was attended by peril, owing to the fact that he was a Protestant and that the Archduke Ferdinand had recently, when on a pilgrimage, vowed he would root out all heretics from his territories and was taking serious steps to give effect to his vow. Kepler thus felt himself faced with banishment if not imprisonment, and Tycho's increasingly urgent letters to him suggesting joint work influenced him.

"Do come," wrote Tycho; "you will find in me a friend who in any emergency will not fail you with help and counsel. But I would not have you driven to seek refuge with me owing to stress of circumstances. I want you to come at the bidding of your own free judgment and because of your love and enthusiasm for the science we both serve." And again: "I write you as a welcoming friend, and as my dearest friend in scanning the heavens as far as the instruments at my disposal permit. And if you come quickly, I will certainly find you a post in which there will be better pay for yourself and your family than you have had hitherto."

Kepler answered these kindly and urgent words without

[175]

committing himself, for he felt none too assured that the decisive step would be a wise one, particularly as he was aware of Tycho's difficult temperament, and of his own frail health. So as to have an additional inducement for Kepler, Tycho availed himself of an audience with the emperor to draw Rudolph's attention to the immense value to Tycho's own work of Kepler's cooperation, and he begged Rudolph to assist by giving Kepler some fitting post with a corresponding salary. Tycho further enlisted the aid of various trusty Prague acquaintances such as the privy councilor, Baron Hoffman, who was already an admirer of Kepler, and of Johannes Homalius and others. The pressure from all sides became so strong that Kepler finally set out for Benatky to give the work at least a trial.

Upon Kepler's arrival in January 1600, Tycho subdivided the Benatky schedule in the following manner: Kepler was to continue his planetary work, devoting his time principally to Mars, Longomontanus was to work on the lunar theory, and Tycho's second son, Jørgen, was to be in charge of the laboratory. To assist further in what now promised to be a period of great accomplishments, Tycho fired off letters to Johannes Müller in Brandenburg, David Fabricius in East Friesland, and Christopher Rothmann in Holstein, asking each of them to come and join him and Kepler. The old fire was flaring up again brightly.

Unfortunately Tycho and Kepler, though both men of genius, were of such hopelessly different temperaments that amicable, daily labor in common was out of the question. Tycho had never worked with equals, only with assistants and pupils whom he had commanded and ordered around as if they were servants. The sensitive, pure and truly noble character of the younger man was wounded by being treated as a beginner and an inferior by the irritable and violent elder, who evidently made no attempt to master his temper. Moreover, the jealous son-in-law to be, Tengnagel, did all in his power to wound the brilliant newcomer. Added to this, the constant hubbub, con-

troversies and excitements of the Benatky household distracted
Kepler, who felt he had fallen among lunatics. He went about
his duties, however, aiding in observations and preparing for the
great work on the planets to which he was later to devote his
life. He likewise agreed to assist Tycho in working on the tables
that were to bear the name of "Rudolphine." Despite his self-
restraint Kepler was, however, slowly being worn down. He
opened his heart in a letter to a friend: "Here I have found
everything insecure. Tycho is a man with whom no one can live
without exposing himself to the greatest indignities. The pay is
splendid, but one can only extract the half of it. I have thought
of turning to medicine. Perhaps you could give me some employment."

At last, unable to stand the situation any longer, Kepler left
for the good Baron Hoffman's in Prague, explaining to him
frankly the whole hopeless situation. The baron and Professor
Jessen put their heads together and were finally able to patch up
matters and induce Kepler to return and give the joint work a
second trial. Tycho, repentant at heart, gave Kepler the warm-
est welcome upon his return, but the attempt was short-lived
owing to Kepler's nervous breakdown.

Kepler evidently needed a good rest; moreover, he had to
straighten out the confused situation of his family at Graz. When
he left for that city he carried Tycho's blessing and a most ap-
preciative letter, and it was understood that when he returned
the entire astronomical establishment might be moved elsewhere, so that its two leaders with their respective families need
not live so closely cooped up together.

After Kepler's departure, various matters, other than the
stars, took up Tycho's attention. First of all, Elisabet's and
Tengnagel's forthcoming wedding had to be celebrated with
proper festivities; then he wished to have himself and his sons
naturalized as Bohemians. But above all he wished to rend the
abhorred imperial mathematician, Ursus, limb from limb. Unable to keep the temporary truce, "the Bear" had once more

attacked Tycho, stating that he would meet him as a bear bereft of its young whelps, and this time ridiculing and making a laughing-stock of him in a public lecture, probably hoping that by so doing he might injure him at court. Bär called Tycho a scientific charlatan, hiding his ignorance under clumsy arrogance, and added "that he made his astronomical observations through his nose, which he used as a sight-vane."

Tycho fairly boiled as he read the lecture, entitled *"Chrono-theatrum,"* in its printed form, which had been circulated among many who had attended it. The fact that Kepler had presented Ursus with a copy of his first publication, a calendar for 1594, came near to causing a serious misunderstanding between the two astronomers. This matter was, however, cleared up, and Tycho wrote Kepler to hurry back and aid him in answering Ursus in a worthy *Apologia Tychonis contra Ursum*, as well as in the preparation of the libel suit he proposed to bring against him. Kepler arrived with wife and stepdaughter and, much against his will, set himself heroically to work on the reply. The enemy's death fortunately ended the bitter conflict.

Happily, Tycho's solicitations to the emperor on behalf of Kepler had not been in vain, for a courier arrived at Benatky with the good news from Baron Hoffman that Kepler had been appointed imperial mathematician with a yearly salary of a hundred thaler.

In asking the emperor for citizenship, Tycho had stated that he did not want to dwell in Bohemia "as a foreigner but as an acknowledged nobleman there." Rudolph had also acted in this matter and written to the Bohemian Estates that he wished "Tycho and his progeny to be included in the country's rolls, according to old custom." Hearing this, Tycho set himself at once to designing a new coat-of-arms to be registered for the purpose. It showed the arms of the Danish Brahes, supported by the astronomical signs for the sun and moon, with a few additional signs to keep them company. Death hindered carrying out the Bohemian naturalization, but Tycho did succeed in having a document published in Prague in which his children were declared legitimate. Whether this was or was not technically correct, Kirstine certainly had earned recognition after twenty-seven years of faithful slavery.

Learning that things were going none too well at Benatky, the emperor purchased the Curtius house in Prague for Tycho, and told him to move temporarily his twenty-eight instruments into the gardens and loggia of the palace of Belvedere or into the Ferdinand Lustschloss.[5] The demon of restlessness again possessing him and being always glad of a change of scene, and particularly so in this instance, Tycho packed up his multifarious paraphernalia and left Benatky, first taking up temporary residence at the Golden Griffin on the Hradschin. But this proved too noisy and distracting. In addition to the courtyard brawls, the ringing of nearby cloister-bells almost drove him crazy. In the records of the adjacent cloister the following entry was made:

"The Emperor wished to drive the Carthusian monks out of Prague owing to the complaint of an alchemist, who because of their presence could accomplish nothing with his sorcery. This alchemist came from a noble Danish family. His name was Tycho Brahe. This alchemist complained of the Carthusians, saying that their prayers and services disturbed him, and the Emperor, who was gullible, thereupon ordered the monks to leave Prague. But the High Chancellor of the kingdom, Herr Ignatz Adalbert Labkowitz, reversed the Emperor's order. In the meantime the Emperor, whenever the Carthusians held prayers, began to have cramps of the heart and had really serious attacks. He knew, however, of no reason for such attacks, which were caused by the sorcery of the aforementioned alchemist, and the matter went so far that the Emperor believed he saw the monks actually in front of him and so he often cried

[5] The only one of the buildings from which Tycho made observations that is still standing is an exquisite Renaissance palace built by Italian workmen under Paolo della Stella, aided by the great Jacobo Sansovino.

out that their banishment must be enforced. When the venerable Father Laurentius of Brindisi heard about these attacks of the Emperor, at such times as the Carthusians held their services, he ordered these held in the evening after *Completoriam*. But it was all in vain, for the Emperor was now plagued by attacks in the evening, just in the same manner he had been during the night, and for the entire winter he never ceased talking about banishment of the Carthusians."

As far as Tycho and the noise were concerned, the affair ended by his moving to his old friend Curtius' house in time for the wedding of his daughter Elisabet with his pupil, the Westphalian nobleman Tengnagel. An observatory was at once installed with wall decorations picturing King Alfonso X, Ptolemy, Charles V, Copernicus, Emperor Rudolph, Frederik II and Tycho himself—all astronomers or patrons of the science.

Though Longomontanus, his faithful pupil of many years, had departed for the University of Copenhagen, where he had just been appointed professor of mathematics, other friends and relatives from all over Europe were invited to the wedding. Fortune seemed again to be smiling on Tycho, and he felt once more like expressing his happy feelings in his customary manner, in Latin verse. His wedding invitations to his intimate old friend, Holger Rosenkrantz, read as follows: "I want to let you know that with God's assistance I intend, sometime between Easter and Pentecost, here in the Curtius house in Prague, where I am living, to give a wedding party for my daughter, the honest and well-born lady, Elisabet Brahe, who is to marry a gentleman of Westphalia, named Franz Tengnagel von Camp. I thus beg you most kindly to come here at the time mentioned and be happy and jolly with the other nobles and good people belonging to His Imperial Majesty's Council, as well as others of this estimable Bohemian kingdom who I hope will turn up at my house for this occasion."

Rosenkrantz could not come, but many others did and the

festivities were highly successful. The celebration over, the household quieted down, and work was recommenced. Every passing trader brought questions from universities, requests for opinions on astronomical or mathematical matters, or for the designs or construction of instruments. Some of the pupils were set to work on the construction of a new armilla, with numerous little carved figures adorning its gilded tripod and at its corners enthroned figurines of the monarchs who had most notably advanced the cause of astronomy—Alfonso X of Spain, Charles V, Rudolph II and Frederik II. The printing presses were busy daily printing completed manuscripts such as Tycho's defense against the Englishman Craigie's attack, and above all the still incomplete first volume of the great work, *Astronomiæ instauratæ progymnasmata*, the second volume of which, as mentioned formerly, had already been printed in Uraniborg under the heading *De mundi ætherii recentioribus phænomenis*.

The tables of stars were so far advanced that Tycho and Kepler requested a joint audience of the emperor to solicit his permission to publish them as the Rudolphine tables.[6] The favor was granted, and Rudolph's name has come down to posterity with an added luster as his reward for his patronage of the two great astronomers of his age.

The longer they worked together, the greater became Tycho's appreciation of his helpmate. He saw at last that Kepler expended his whole personality, heart and head alike, upon their work, and that to him life held nothing but white-hot, liberating, up-striving labor. Kepler had the immortal fire that nothing could quench, and it is to Tycho's everlasting glory that, despite his widely different nature, he came to realize the greatness of his associate.

[6] The tables, which were originally intended to be part of the *Progymnasmata*, finally appeared in 1627.

CHAPTER ELEVEN

When I consider thy heavens, the work of thy fingers, the moon and the stars which thou hast ordained. . . .—
PSALM 8:3

CHAPTER ELEVEN

TYCHO had never taken any care of his health or
done anything beyond having an absurd occasional consultation with doctors as to his trouble
with his bladder. He had never paid any attention to the advice he had received or remembered to take any of the precautions prescribed.

In the month of October 1601, he was invited by his friend,
Baron Peter Vok von Rosenberg, to dine. As usual, Tycho had
forgotten to take any precautions before leaving home, and during the meal he drank copiously. "Then," says the old account,
"Owing to the strict etiquette of the day he did not like to leave
the table, and in staying burst something of importance inside
his lower regions. When he was able to totter up it was too late,
the harm was done, and his bladder was wronged beyond repair."

He was brought home to the Curtius house and doctors and
imperial officials hurried to his bedside to wag their wise heads,
prescribe powders and medicaments and a diet, most of which
the poor, obstreperous sufferer still had strength and wisdom
enough to refuse to submit to. In the following days of agony he
repeated several times to those making his breathing more difficult by crowding around his bedside: *"Ne frustra vixisse
videar!"* ("I hope I will not appear to have lived in vain.")

His son Tyge was away in Italy, but Jørgen and Kepler were
there, and he begged them to remain faithful to their studies.
He turned to Kepler in particular, beseeching him to finish the
Rudolphine tables as soon as possible, and expressing the hope
that in developing his theory of the universe he would base it
on the Tychonian rather than the Copernican system. During
his stay, the wise and gentle Kepler had time and again had the
good sense to fight shy of all discussion of the system of the

planets on which the two disagreed so basically. Now that he saw the master's work was finished, he merely acquiesced.

Tycho died on October 24, 1601, after eleven days of illness. He had by his labors supplied a sure foundation for modern astronomy, and had given his great associate the means of continuing the work that was commenced by Copernicus and was to be completed by Newton.

Emperor Rudolph was as distressed by Tycho's death as his curious, half-rational nature allowed. He ordered a magnificent funeral for his imperial astronomer to be held in the Teyn Church. He likewise announced that he would shoulder the greater portion of the expense for, as he explained to his councilors, he wished Tycho Brahe buried "in an honorable manner." Says one old account: "At the funeral the streets were so crowded that the procession walked between the people as between two walls. The church was so full of counts, countesses, ladies, and many others, both nobles and commoners, that you could scarcely squeeze your way in." And another account relates that "the funeral procession was headed by persons carrying candles decorated with the Brahe family arms. Next followed a banner of black damask with the arms and name of the deceased embroidered in gold. Then came his [Tycho's] favorite horse, succeeded by another banner and a second horse, after which came persons bearing a helmet with feathers in the family colors, a pair of gilt spurs, and a shield with the Brahe coat-of-arms. Then came the coffin, covered with a velvet cloth on which lay Tycho's spurs and sword. This was carried by twelve imperial gentlemen-at-arms. Tycho had been laid out in full armor as befitted his rank. Directly behind the coffin came the younger son, walking between Count Erik Brahe and the imperial chancellor, Ernfried Minkowitz, and followed by councilors and nobles. Then came the widow, walking between two gentlemen of exalted rank, followed by her four daughters, Magdalene, Elisabet Tengnagel, Sofie and the youngest,

Cecilie, similarly attended, and the pupils, swathed in long mourning clothes."

Tycho's faithful Wittenberg companion, Professor Johannes Jessen, delivered the funeral oration,[1] and, true to their old friendship, did not stint his eloquence. He said, after a slight reference to Tycho's nose, or rather lack of it, and the calumnies of his arch-enemy, Ursus (Bär): "I do not, however, make a God of Tycho Brahe, but acknowledge that he had his faults, from which no man is free. But I can bear witness to the fact that during the nine months which he and his family spent with me in Wittenberg, he behaved as a Christian and a learned man should have towards God and his fellow men. He lived in perfect agreement with his wife and he kept his children in the fear of God and the pursuit of virtue. He made his sons study and his daughters keep busy in household duties. No one was permitted to be idle. He was friendly to strangers and charitable to the poor. His words were brief and truthful, his counsel wise, his acts fortunate. He was neither hypocritical nor false, but he spoke out plainly, which earned him the hatred of many. He coveted nothing but time. He endeavored to serve everyone and hurt no one. He always spoke the truth. Science was his passion, his sufficiency and his riches. Virtue was his nobility, religion his pleasure. He harbored no grudge, but forgave everyone."[2]

On his tombstone was cut *"Non fasces nec opes sola artis, sceptra perennant,"* the motto that he had early taken as his guide.

When Kirstine in 1604 followed Tycho to the grave, only three years later, she was buried beside him, and the children erected an imposing monument over them with a full-length, standing figure of Tycho in armor, his left hand on his sword,

---

[1] Funeral orators were very well paid, generally by a heavy silver tankard or twenty daler, if the deceased was of rank or importance.

[2] Johannes Jessen, *De vita et morte D. Tychonis Brahei. Oratio funebris. . . .* Prague, 1601. See Bibliography.

his right on a globe, surmounting the arms of Bille and Brahe and those of his two grandmothers, Ulfstand and Rud.[3]

Tycho had held the fief of Hveen for life. This now reverted to the Crown, and King Christian gave it to Cort Barleben. In 1616 Hveen was given to Karen Andersdatter, then the latest of the king's mistresses.[4] He had met her at a wedding party where he became so enamored of her that he insisted upon taking her home with him to the palace. Her betrothed, Niels Glostrup, though temporarily disconcerted, was more than placated by being given the Køge vicarage and later being made bishop of Oslo, receiving into the bargain Karen's sister, Anna, for his wife. Christian always did things handsomely!

While Hveen in Tycho's day had been considered an appendix to Sjælland, it was subsequently placed under the jurisdic-

[3] In 1901, curiosity and interest prompted the Czechs to exhume the remains of Tycho and Kirstine. They were remarkably well preserved by embalming. Tycho's body was intact with the exception of the gold and silver nose, which the grave-diggers, or whoever saw the last of him, evidently decided would profit them more than it would the deceased. A portion of Tycho's skull had been broken by the falling of the masonry of the vault. The Viennese newspaper, the *Neue Freie Presse*, gave the following account of the disinterment: "On the occasion of the 300th anniversary of Tycho Brahe's death the Prague Town Council decided to assemble the remains of the celebrated astronomer, which lay in the Teyn Church, and bury them anew. The work was commenced yesterday and superintended by Mr. Herlein. After having lifted the stone block of the monument, situated near the first column in the nave, which supported a full length effigy of the great astronomer, a semi-collapsed arch was discovered, and on removing the stones two moldering coffins were seen. On the following day a committee met to determine whether the bodies they contained were those of Tycho Brahe and his wife. Two workmen with candles descended into the vault and removed the rubbish which covered the coffins, the wood of which was quite rotten and fell into pieces at any rough touch. At 10 a.m. the lid of the first coffin was free to be removed. A surprising sight met the eye. The body in the coffin resembled the effigy on the monument to an extraordinary degree. The head was slightly turned to one side, the bones of the face and the peaked Spanish beard were well preserved. The head was covered by a skull-cap, and the neck surrounded by a Spanish ruff, which, like the remainder of the clothing, had suffered little during the 300 years since Tycho Brahe was laid in his last resting place. The feet were shod in long cavalry boots reaching up over the knees. That the body was Tycho Brahe's was also proved by the absence of the nose. Tycho lost this organ in a duel and wore a silver one in its place. Among the rubbish was found a silver wreath and a spray of flowers. The construction of the grave was rather remarkable, the stones being set loosely over one another. This was all the more astounding as Tycho Brahe was buried with great pomp and circumstance, but the vault may possibly have been crushed during the reconstruction of the church in 1721."

[4] Karen bore the king a son and two daughters.

tion of the court of justice at Lund in Scania, owing to the complaints of the island's inhabitants about the long distance to the Sjælland court. Then, by the humiliating treaty of Roskilde in 1658, Denmark's provinces east of the Sound were ceded to the Swedish king, Carl Gustaf, and with them went the island of Hveen, since it was under Lund.

Hveen shimmers today, as it did in the sixteenth century, in the changing gray lights of the Sound, but its fairy-tale castle has vanished. However, a record of its wonders remains to us in the reproductions of the buildings and their instruments, engraved and printed in the books and pamphlets from Tycho's presses that still can be found in the world's libraries and museums.

Tycho has been reproached because, fifty years after Copernicus had worked out a planetary system, he championed one that represented a step backward instead of forward. It has been said that he thus failed to influence the development of astronomic thought. True enough, the system which we accept today is named the Copernican. But its present form is very different in detail from that which was set up by the genius whose name it bears.

Properly weighed and valued, Tycho Brahe's achievements were, nevertheless, such that he ranks today as one of the two or three greatest scientists ever produced by the North-European countries. The treasure trove of his observations of the moon and planets exceeds even his determination of the positions of a thousand fixed stars. He was a link in the great chain: Copernicus, Brahe, Kepler, Galileo, Newton.

Tycho's weaknesses were painfully evident, for they lay on the surface: he was unapproachable, irritable, unsparing and even vengeful, but he was also a spiritual aristocrat and a true friend. He all but broke down under the burden of the manifold contradictions of his nature. Kepler said of him when he died that he possessed riches he had never utilized. He protested against most contemporaneous opinions, by his marriage, by

disbelief in the devil worship of the time, by favoring the introduction of the Gregorian calendar, by condemnation of the life
of his social equals. He felt there was only one way to know the
truth and that was to sweep aside all the dark cobwebs of old
sophistry. He was an independent thinker, and his belief in his
own genius remained with him until his dying day.

Dreyer, the Scottish biographer of Tycho, says of him: "He
not only conceived the necessity of supplying materials for
discovery of the true motions of the heavenly bodies, and by
his improvement of instruments and accumulation of observations, made it possible for Kepler to reach his goal, but in almost
all the branches of practical and spherical astronomy he opened
new paths, and made the first serious advance since the days of
the Alexandrine school."[5] Further, "And excluding the hypothesis respecting the arrangement of the solar system, which
never had any followers, and which coming after Copernicus
is considered a retrograde step, and considering the extent, accuracy and importance of Tycho Brahe's observations, and the
results to which they led, we can conclude that there is no observer, ancient or modern, whose labors have produced a more
marked influence on the progress of astronomy."

Fortunately, Tycho was a radical in his scientific work.
Though he published but four major books, that on the star in
Cassiopeia, his book on Hveen and its instruments, his letters,
and the second volume of *Astronomiæ instauratæ progymnasmata*,[6] these were epochal, and the vast amount of data and
notes and observations he left behind him were bequeathed to
and benefited posterity through the labors of his great pupil.

One might speculate that it was fortunate for science that
Tycho left Denmark instead of continuing his great work there
until his death. For had not the results of his work fallen into
Kepler's hands, enabling him to work out his own laws with
their aid, Tycho's findings would probably have remained bur-

[5] J. L. E. Dreyer, *Tycho Brahe.* . . . Edinburgh, 1890, p. 363.
[6] See Bibliography.

ied for many a decade. They formed the basis of Kepler's discoveries and of the Rudolphine tables. Finding through Tycho's enormous labor that the planets' orbits are ellipses, of which the sun is in one focus, and that, as the planet describes its orbit, its radius vector traverses equal areas in equal time, Kepler supplied the groundwork for Newton's discoveries, the starting point of modern astronomy.

Kepler was not only a great mathematician, but inventive, full of original ideas and exceedingly productive. In his work with Tycho, one does not know which to admire the more, Kepler's patience or his penetration.

The different mentalities of the two men led each one along his own line. Kepler's unlimited speculative propensity supplemented Tycho's mechanical faculty. He found in Tycho's ample legacy of first-class data precisely what enabled him to try, by the touchstone of fact, the successive hypotheses that he postulated. Kepler's untiring patience in comparing and calculating the observations at his disposal was rewarded by his revolutionary findings.

No more congruous arrangement could have been devised than the inheritance by Kepler of the wealth of materials amassed by Tycho. The younger man's genius supplied what was wanting in his predecessor. Tycho's endowments were of a practical order, yet he had never designed his observations to be an end in themselves.

After Tycho Brahe's death Kepler forgot all his difficulties with him and only remembered the gratitude he owed him for a great heritage. In his writings he never omitted to do honor to the man without whose labors he probably would never have found out the secrets of the planetary motions. He never mentioned him without the greatest respect and admiration for his investigations and theories, and this despite the fact that he himself had taken a very different scientific road. The mighty impulse Tycho Brahe and Johann Kepler gave to astronomy caused the science to be taken up at the universities, and among them Copenhagen and Leyden were the first to found observatories.

In his *Astronomiæ instauratæ mechanica* Tycho wrote that he considered his Hveen accomplishments to be "the improved elements of the solar orbit, the discovery of a new inequality in the moon's motion, the variability of the inclination of the lunar orbit and the motion of the nodes, the observation of accurate positions of a thousand fixed stars, the explosion of the time-honored error about the irregularity in the procession of the equinoxes, the accumulation of a vast mass of carefully planned observations of the planets, in order to have new tables of their motions constructed, and the observations of comets, proving them to be much farther from the earth than the moon." This was indeed a record of gigantic achievement, which, if only Denmark had recognized its value and size, would have made her forgive Tycho's shortcomings and consider only the extraordinary fruits of his genius and tireless energy.

APPENDIX

*Brief Account of Tycho Brahe's Offspring**

1. *Kirstine*, b. Oct. 1573, d. Sept. 1576. Buried in Helsingborg. On the epitaph was inscribed *filiola naturalis*.
2. *Magdalene*, b. 1574 in Copenhagen at the time Tycho was lecturing at the University there (autumn 1574 until early 1575).
3. *Elisabet*, no dates seem to be available.
4. *Claudius*, b. Jan. 6, 1577. Died six days later.
5. *Sofie*, b. Aug. 4, 1578.
6. *Tyge*, b. Aug. 1581.
7. *Jørgen*, b. 1583.
8. *Cecilie*, date of birth unknown.

Of his eight children six survived. They and their mother Kirstine came away with him to Prague, and were all near him when he died (Oct. 24, 1601) except the eldest son, Tyge, who was in Italy at the time. His wife survived him by only three years. She died in 1604. As to the further fate of Tycho's offspring little is known.

Magdalene, after her unfortunate engagement to Gellius Sascerides, never married.

Elisabet married Tycho's assistant, Franz Ganzneb Tengnagel, who had come with him to Prague. She died in 1613 leaving several children. Her husband died in 1622.

Sofie did not marry. Her brother Jørgen with whom in 1636 she spent some time in Prague in quest of payment of money owed them by the state, said of her: "As to Sofie, her thought stumbled and she became feebleminded. She turned to Catholicism." (A remark that probably must be seen against the background of the religious war then raging.)

* Principally based on material in J. L. E. Dreyer, *Tycho Brahe*. . . . Edinburgh, 1890. P. 72-73.

Tyge married in Bohemia in 1604. He had five children. He died on September 2, 1627.

Jørgen, who was called Georg in Bohemia, died in 1640 near Pürglitz. He seems to have been very active in his endeavors to obtain payment for Tycho's instruments sold to Rudolph II, for 20,000 thalers of which only 5,000 were paid.

Cecilie married the Swedish baron Gustaf Sparre. She died in Cracow, Poland.

Neither Tyge nor Jørgen appear to have taken much interest in astronomy. But their father often used them as messengers and couriers, and so they were acquainted with his colleagues and correspondents. After his death they apparently spent an inordinate amount of time trying to make the state coffers of Bohemia pay out the rest of the amount of 15,000 thalers, but with scant success, wars and hard times intervening. On May 23, 1614 King Mathias of Bohemia acknowledged in writing "the debt of 15,000 good silver thalers of Prague" to Tyge, Jørgen (Georg), Magdalene, Sofie, Elisabet and Cecilie. Only a small part of the money was ever paid to them. All through their lives there had been doubt as to whether Tycho's offspring were legitimate, their mother being of peasant stock. In 1630 their fine Aunt Sofie who had always stood by Tycho and his family, certified a document to the effect that all of Tycho's children were born in wedlock and, consequently, were his legitimate offspring and heirs.

BIBLIOGRAPHY

Becket, Francis and Christensen, Charles. Uraniborg og
Stjerneborg. København, A. Marcus, 1921.

Behring Liisberg, H. C. København i gamle Dage og Livet i
København. Kobenhavn, H. Hagerup, 1901.

Brahe, Tychonis. De nova stella. Hafniæ, Lorentz Benedict,
1573. 52 pp.

————. Horoscopus Sr. Regis Christiani IV-ti, ad mandatum
Sr. Regis Friederici II-di, a Tychone Brahe Ottonide con-
script. in Insula Hvena. Cal. Julii Ao. 1577 [Tycho's horoscopes—themata genethliaca—of the royal princes Christian,
Ulrik and Hans, Frederik II's sons are printed in *Opera
omnia*, I.]

————. Observationes cometæ anni 1585, Uraniburg habitæ a
T. Brahe. [Gellius Sascerides—pupil of Tycho—made copies
of the book on the comet for distribution. They were ready in
1588, but not for sale until 1603.]

————. Poems in Latin to Jacob Ulfeld; Hans Frandsen (Joannis Francisci Ripensis); Niels Kaas; Henrik Rantzau were
printed at Uraniborg, 1585.

————. De mundi ætherii recentioribus phænomenis. Liber
secundus, Uraniborg, 1588. [Printer] Weida. Colophon:
"Suspiciendo despicio." [Reprint] Frankfurt, G. Tampach-
ius, 1610. [This is part II of Tycho's *Astronomiæ instauratæ
progymnasmata*. Part I was published after Tycho's death in
Opera omnia edited by Johann Kepler, Prag, 1602. Vols. II-
IV. In Part I, besides a reprint of *De nova stella*, there is a
catalogue of 777 stars to which Johann Kepler added 228.
The catalogue of stars will be found in Vol. III of *Opera omnia*, and in Memoirs of the Royal Astronomical Society, Vol.
XIII, edited by Baily. Part II contains observations about the
comet of 1577.]

————. Elegia ad Daniam. Wandesburgi, 1593.

————. Epistolæ astronomicæ, Uraniburgum 1596. [Corre-
spondence with Landgrave William IV of Hesse-Cassel and
his astronomer Christopher Rothmann.] 176 pp.

————. Icones instrumentorum quorundam astronomiæ in-
staurandæ gratia. Uraniburgum, 1596.

————. Astronomiæ instauratæ mechanica. Wandesburgi,
1598. [Reprinted in Nuremberg in 1602, by Levin Hulsius,
exact copy of original text. The most important instruments
described in it are: Quadrans muralis sive Tychonis; Quadrans azimuthalis; Sextans trigonicus; Armillæ æquatoriæ
maximæ; Pinnacidier. Details in *Opera omnia*, v. An English translation by Hans Ræder and Bengt Strömgren was
published at Copenhagen in 1946: Tycho Brahe's description
of his instruments and scientific work.]

————. De disciplinis mathematices oratio publica recitata in
Academia Haffniensi anno 1574 et nunc primum edita. . . .
Opera Conradi Aslaci Bergensis, Hafniæ, 1610. [Tycho lec-
tured at the Copenhagen University from September 23,
1574, until the early part of 1575. These lectures were
printed after his death by his pupil Konrad Axelsen from
Bergen (Conradus Aslacus Bergensis), and dedicated to
Tycho's brother, Steen Brahe.]

Brahe, Tychonis Dani—*Opera omnia*. Edidit I. L. E. Dreyer
Hauniæ, Libraria Gyldendaliana 1913-1929. 15 vols. Auspiciis Societatis linguæ et litterarum Danicarium. Tomus 1-5:
Scripta astronomica, edidit Dreyer auxilio I. [Hans] Ræder,
sumptus fecit G. A. Hagemann, 1913-1923. Tomus 6-8:
Epistolæ astronomicæ, edidit Dreyer auxilio I. Ræder, sumptus fecit G. A. Hagemann, 1919-1925. Tomus 9: Scripta
varia, ediderunt Dreyer et I. Ræder, sumptus fecit Institutum
Rask Oerstedianium, 1924. Tomus 10-13: Thesaurus obser-
vationum ad fidem codicum primum integrum, edidit Dreyer;
sumptibus Institutei Carlsbergici, 1923-1926. Tomus 14:
Epistolæ et acta ad vitam Tychonis Brahei pertinentia, edidit
E. Nystrøm, sumptus fecit Institutum Rask Oerstedianum,

1928. Tomus 15: Index hominum et rerum—Confecerunt I. L. E. Dreyer et I. Ræder—præmissa est carminum appendix, sumptus fecerunt Institutum Carlsbergicum & Institutum Rask Oerstedianum, 1929.

Brandi, Karl. The emperor Charles V, the growth and destiny of a man and of a world empire. Translated from the German by C. V. Wedgwood. London, J. Cape, 1939.

Brewster, Sir David. The martyrs of science; or the lives of Galileo, Tycho Brahe and Kepler. New York, Harper & Brothers, 1841. [Later editions 1870, 1872.]

Bricka, C. F. En dansk Adelsmands Udtalelser om Tycho Brahe. København, Danske Magazin, Ser. v, Vol. 1, 1887-1889.

Burckhardt, F. Aus Tycho Brahes Briefwechsel. Basel, 1887.

————. Zur Erinnerung an Tycho Brahe, 1546-1601. Basel, Georg & Co., 1901.

Charlier, C. V. L. Utgräfningarna af Tycho Brahes observatorier på ön Hven sommeren 1901. I festskrift från kungl. Fysiografiska Sällskapet i Lund i anledning af 300-årsdagen af Tycho Brahes död. Lund, 1901.

Danske Magazin. [Various articles on Tycho Brahe.] København. Ser. ii, Vol. 1; Ser. iii, Vols. 4 and 5; Ser. iv, Vol. 2. 1854-1857.

Delambre, Jean Baptiste J. Histoire de l'astronomie moderne. 1. Paris, 1821.

Dreyer, J. L. E. Tycho Brahe, a picture of scientific life and work in the sixteenth century. Edinburgh, A. & C. Black, 1890.

————. Tycho Brahes Fortjenester af Astronomien. En populær Fremstilling. København, G. E. C. Gad, 1901.

Dvorsky, Franz. Nové zpravý o Tychony Brahova a jehs rodinê. Prague, Casopis Musea Královstvi českévo. 1883, 1901. [New contributions to the history of Tycho Brahe and his family. Bulletin of the Royal Bohemian National Museum.]

Favaro, A. Carteggio inedito di Ticone Brahei . . . con Giovanni Magini. Bologna, 1886.

Faxe, W. Fornlämningar af Tycho Brahes Stjerneborg och Uranienborg på ön Hven aftäckte åren 1823 och 1824. Stockholm, 1824.

Flemløs, Peder Jacobsen. En Elementisch eller Jordisch Astrologia om Luftens Forendring. Tilsammendragen aff Peder Jacobsen Flemløs paa Hueen. Prentit paa Uraniborg Aff Hans Gaschitz, Anno 1591. xvi, 143 pp. [This is the book of 399 short rules to foretell the weather, for instance, by noticing the behavior of animals. Reprinted at Copenhagen in 1644, by Longomontanus.]

Fredericia, J. A. and Pechüle, C. F. Tyge Brahe. København, 1901.

Friis, Frederik Reinholdt. Tychonis Brahei Dani observationes septem cometarum. Hafniæ, 1867. [Tycho Brahe's observations of seven comets, edited by F. R. Friis.]

————. Tyge Brahe. En historisk Fremstilling efter trykte og utrykte Kilder. København, 1871.

————. Breve og Aktstykker angaaende Tyge Brahe og hans Slægtninge. (Samlede af F. R. Friis.) København, 1875.

————. Brahe, Tycho. 1546-1601. Tychonis Brahei et ad eum doctorum virorum epistolæ nunc primum collectæ et editæ a F. R. Friis. Hafniæ, G. E. C. Gad, 1876-1902. Vol. I in 4 parts 1876-1886; ab 1568-1587. Vol. II incomplete in 11 parts 1900-1909; ab 1588- .

————. Minder om Tycho Brahes Ophold i Bøhmen. H. Scharlings Tidsskrift for Kirke og Folkeliv, Literatur og Kunst. København. Vol. I, p. 225 ff.; Vol. II, p. 257 ff. [About Tycho's death, sale of his instruments and his children's efforts to obtain payment.]

————. Nogle Efterretninger om Tyge Brahe og hans Familie. København, G. E. C. Gad, 1902.

————. Peder Jacobsen Flemløs. Tyge Brahes første Medhjælper og hans Observationer i Norge. København, G. E. C. Gad, 1905.

——. Sofie Brahe Ottesdatter. København, G. E. C. Gad, 1905.

Gassendi, Pierre (Petro). Institutio astronomica juxta hypothesis tam veterum quam Copernici et Tychonis;—Oratio inauguralis iterato, edit. Lundini, 1653.

——. Tychonis Brahei vita, accessit Nicolai Copernici, Georgii Peurbachii et Joannis Regimontani vita. Parisiis, 1654.

Gray, R. A. The Life and Work of Tycho Brahe. Journal of the Royal Astronomical Society of Canada. March, April 1923. Vol. XVII.

Hasner, Dr. Joseph von. Tycho Brahe und Kepler in Prag. Prag, 1872.

Helfrecht, Johann Theodor Benjamin. Tycho Brahe, geschildert nach seinem Leben. Hof, 1798.

Hemmingsen, Niels. Om Æcteskab. København, 1562.

Hofman, T. de. Portraits historiques des hommes illustres de, Danemark. Copenhague, 1746. [Part 6 covers Tycho B.]

Holberg, Ludvig. Dannemarks riges historie. Deelt udi 3 tomer. Ny Udgave udgivet af I. Levin. København, A. F. Høst, 1856.

Jessen, Johannes. De vita et morte D. Tychonis Brahe. Oratio Funebris D. Joannis Jessenii. Pragæ, 1601. Hamburgi 1610. [Jessen's funeral oration, also reprinted by Gassendi in his life of Tycho Brahe, pp. 224-235.]

Kepler, Johann: Omnia opera Tychonis Brahei. Tychonis Brahe Dani *Astronomiæ instauratæ progymnasmata*. Quorum hæc prima pars de restitutione motuum solis & lunæ, stellarumque inerrantium tractat. Et præterea de admiranda nova stella anno 1572 exorta luculenter agit. Typis inchoata Uraniburgi Daniæ, absoluta Pragæ Bohemiæ MDCII (1602) [1,500 copies were sold to bookseller and editor Gottfried Tampach in Frankfurt. New issue by him in 1610.]

[Vol. II of Progymnasmata printed at Uraniborg in 1588 was published with a new title page and dedication to the Imperial Secretary in Prague, Barwitz, by Tycho's son-in-law, Franz Tengnagel, in 1603. New edition in 1610.]

Kuylenstierna-Wenster, Elisabeth. Sophie Ottosdotter: Berättelsen om et kvinnoöde. Stockholm, C. E. Fritze, 1910.

Langebek. Collection of letters, royal decrees and documents. Danske Magazin, Copenhagen, 1746. Vol. II.

Lauritzen, P. Danske Mænd, Tyge Brahe. København, 1925.

Mengel, Christian Gottlob. Lebensbeschreibung des berühmten und gelehrten dänischen Sternsehers Tycho Brahe, aus der dänische Sprache in die deutsche übersetzt—von Philander von der Weistritz. Kopenhagen, F. C. Pelt, 1756.

Mortensen, Harald. Tycho Brahe Minder i Skaane. Stockholm, Særtryk af Svenska Turistföreningens årsskrift, 1926.

———. Tycho Brahe Minder i Prag. Lund, Cassiopeja, 1942.

———. Nicolaus Raimarus Ursus. Lund, Cassiopeja, 1943.

———. Tycho Brahe-Portrætter. Lund, Cassiopeja, 1946.

Nellemann, J. Om Ægteskab, Forlovelse, etc. [Article in] Historisk Tidsskrift, Ser. v, Vol. 1. København, 1879.

Nicolaisen, N. A. Møller: Tycho Brahes Papirmølle paa Hven. København, 1946.

Nielsen, Lauritz. Tycho Brahes Bogtrykkeri paa Hveen. København, 1946. (Article in "Nordisk Tidsskrift for Bog- og Biblioteksvæsen," Vol. 8.)

Nielsen, N. Tycho Brahe og hans Søster. Hillerød, 1934.

Nielsen, Dr. O. Kjøbenhavns Historie. Vols. I-VI. København, 1877-1892.

Nordlind, Wilhelm. Ur Tycho Brahes Brevväxling. Från Latinet. Lund, C. W. K. Gleerups Förlag, 1926.

Noyes, Alfred. The Torch-Bearers. London, W. Blackwood & Sons, 1922.

Nyström, Eiler. Tycho Brahes Brud med Fædrelandet. Festskrift til Kr. Erslev. København, 1927.

Olsen, Elias Cimber Morsing. [Latin: Elias Olai Cimber.] Diarium astrologicum et meteorologicum anni a nato Christo 1586. Et de cometa quodam rotunido omnique cauda destituto qui anno proxime elapso, mensibus Octobri et Nouembri conspiciebatur, ex observationibus certis desumta consideratio astrologica. Per Eliam Olai Cimbrum nobili viro Tychoni Brahe in Astronomicis exercitiies inserventem. Excusum in Officina Uraniburgica, 1587. [Elias Olsen Cimber Morsing stayed at Hveen as Tycho's assistant from 1583 until 1597.]

[The diary was published in Copenhagen in 1876 under the auspices of the Royal Danish Academy of Sciences and Letters.] Tyge Brahes meterologiske Dagbog holdt paa Uraniborg for Aarene 1582-1597. *Appendice* aux *Collecteana meteorologica* publiés sous les auspices de l'Académie Royale des Sciences et des Lettres à Copenhague. 263 pp. Copenhague, 1876.

Olsson, Martin. Svenska Fornminnesplatser: Uraniborg og Stierneborg paa ön Ven. Stockholm, Wahlström & Widstrands Förlag, 1926.

Østergaard, Vilhelm. Tyge Brahe. København, Gyldendal. [A novel.]

Pedersen, P. Den danske Astronom Tycho Brahe. København, 1838.

Petersen, A. Tyge Brahe. København, 1924.

Petersen, E. Om Stjærnetydning og Stjærnekundskab. København, 1885.

Ponsonby, Arthur and Dorothea. Rebels and reformers. Biographies for young people. London, G. Allen & Unwin, 1917.

Prandtl, W. Die Bibliothek des Tycho Brahes. Wien, 1933.

Ræder, Hans and Strömgren, Bengt. Tycho Brahe's description of his instruments and scientific work. Translation of *Astronomiæ instauratæ mechanica*, Wandesburgi, 1598. København, 1946.

Resenii, P. J. Inscriptiones Hafnienses, Stellaburgenses, Urani-
burgenses. Hafniæ, 1668.

Royal Danish Academy of Sciences and Letters. See *Olsen*.

Rørdam, Holger Fr. Kjøbenhavns Universitets Historie. i-iv.
København, 1869-1874.

————. Historiske Samlinger og Studier. i-iv. København,
1891-1902.

————Bidrag til Tycho Brahes Historie. Danske Magazin,
Ser. iv, Vol. 2, København.

Salmonsens Konversations Leksikon, Vol. 3. København, J. H.
Schultz, 1915.

Sand, M. J. Tycho Brahe und seine Sternwarten auf Hven.
Kopenhagen, 1904.

Scaliger, Joseph Justus. Opum novum de emendatione temporum. Leyden, 1583. [About the Gregorian calendar reform.]

Skov, Sigvard. Dansk Videnskab af Verdensry. København,
1944.

Strömgren, Bengt. See *Ræder*.

Thiele, T. N. Tyge Brahes Forhold til sine Konger og sin Videnskab. København, 1901.

Tycho Brahe-Sälskapets Årsbok: Cassiopeja. Lund, 1946. [The
Yearbook "Cassiopeja" of the Swedish Tycho Brahe Society.]

Ursi, Nicolai Reymari (Dithmarsi): Fundamentum astronomicum, Strassburg, 1588. [Nicolai Reymers Bär—Latin:
Ursus—a native of Ditmarschen, and an early pupil of Tycho's.]

Wedgwood, Cicely Veronica. The thirty years war. New Haven,
Yale University Press, 1939.

Weistritz, Philander v.d. (See *Mengel*.) Leben des berühmten
Sternsehers Tycho v. Brahe. ii. Kopenhagen und Leipzig,
1756.

Werlauff, E. C. De Hellige Tre Kongers Kapel i Roskilde
Domkirke. København, 1849.

Westergren, Nils. Tyko Brahe, till 350-årsminnet. Landskrona, A.-B. Gustavsons bokhandel, 1926.

William (Wilhelm) IV, Landgrave of Hesse Cassel. Coeli & siderum in eo errantium observationes Hassicæ illustrissimi Principis Wilhelmi Hassicæ, lantgravi auspiciis quondam institutæ. Et Spicilegium biennale ex observationibus Bohemicis V. N. Tychonis Brahe. Nunc primum publicante Willebrordo Snellio . . . Quibus accesserunt, Ioannis Regiomontani & Bernardi Walteri observationes Noribergicæ. Lugduni Batavorum: Apud Iustum Colsterum, 1618.

Wormii, O. et doctorum virorum ad eum epistolæ, Hafniæ, 1751. [References to Tycho's dwarf, Jeppe, are found in the letters of the Danish physician, Ole Worm.]

INDEX

Abraham, 17
Akerhus, 86, 119
Albattani, 68
Albert, Duke of Prussia, 24
Alfonso X, of Spain, 68, 180, 181
Alkmar, 146
Amager, 29
Amsterdam, 162
Andersdatter, Karen, 188
Andersen, Hans Christian, 71
Anna, Princess, 118, 119
Antvortskov, Castle of, 75
Antwerp, 55, 63, 66
Apollonius, 92
Archimedes, 92, 163
Aristotle, 92, 163
Aslacus, Conradus, 53, 88
Athyn, Bryn, 134
Augsburg, 36, 37, 38, 40, 41, 42, 55, 56, 65, 70, 84, 127, 128, 133, 161, 162
Aurifaber, J., 87
Austria, Anne of, 26
Axelsen, Konrad, 53, 88

Bacon, 7, 15
Bachmeister, 34, 105
Barleben, Cort, 188
Barvetius, 169, 173
Basel, 19, 20, 103, 141
Baza, Theodore, 44
Benatky, 171, 172, 176, 178, 179
Benedict, Lorenzo, 145
Bergen, 3, 60, 88, 93
Bertelsen, 142
Bille, Eske, 71, 145
Bille, 11, 163
Bille, Steen, 28, 29, 36, 39, 40, 46, 47, 58, 99, 110, 118, 128
Blekinge, 3
Blotius, Hugo, 92, 93
Bohemia, 178, 194
Bologna, 19, 26
Bongarcius, J., 93, 105
Brahe, Axel, 137
Brahe, Beate, 13
Brahe, Cecilie, 187, 193, 194
Brahe, Claudius, 193
Brahe, Ebba, 11
Brahe, Elisabet, 88, 177, 180, 186, 193, 194
Brahe, Erik, 186
Brahe, Inger, 14

Brahe, Jørgen, 13, 14, 28, 29, 99, 134, 176
Brahe, Jørgen, Tycho's son, 185, 193, 194
Brahe, Karen, 113, 188
Brahe, Kirstine, 47, 48, 49, 53, 86, 131, 179, 187, 188, 193
Brahe, Kirstine, Tycho's daughter, 47, 193
Brahe, Knud, 13, 62, 99
Brahe, Magdalene, 55, 85, 87, 141, 142, 144, 186, 193, 194
Brahe, Magnus, 11
Brahe, Niels, 11
Brahe, Otto, 12, 13, 14, 59, 70, 99
Brahe, Per, 11
Brahe, Sofie, 47, 48, 88, 89, 131, 140, 142, 186, 193, 194
Brahe, Steen, 13, 123, 137, 164
Brahe, Tyge, 162, 173, 193, 194
Branderburg, Elector of, 152, 160, 176
Brantome, 7
Brasch, 105
Breslau, 88, 92
Brindisi, 179
Brucæus, Heinrich, 34, 100, 105, 151, 162
Bruno, Giordano, 7
Brunswick, 134, 158
Brunswick, Duke of, 118, 121
Brussels, 158
Buchanan, 105, 120
Bugenhagen, 5, 15
Busch, 44
Bygholm, 99

Caesar, Julius, 42
Calvin, 7, 44
Camerarius, Joachim, 22
Caraducius, 162, 165
Carl Gustof, King, 189
Caroline of Hesse-Cassel, 104
Cervantes, 7
Charles V, 7, 26, 37, 158, 169, 181
Charles Vasa, 78
Christian I, 15, 124
Christian III, 4, 153
Christian IV, 3, 4, 38, 60, 75, 77, 101, 102, 108, 112, 113, 117, 118, 121, 124, 126, 131, 138, 144, 145, 150, 152, 154, 157, 161, 164, 174, 188
Christian V, 103
Chytræus, David, 34, 104, 151

Cimber, E. O., 87, 101, 128
Cimber, J. B., 87
Cimber, J. H., 87
Coll, Hans, 87
Collingensis, 87
Cologne, Elector of, 160
Condés, 5
Copenhagen, 3, 18, 26, 27, 29, 37, 39,
  40, 42, 44, 45, 47, 48, 53, 56, 57,
  58, 61, 75, 82, 91, 92, 100, 102,
  105, 106, 109, 117, 118, 119, 128,
  132, 134, 141, 142, 143, 149, 150,
  151, 155, 192
Copenhagen, Castle of, 154, 157
Copenhagen, University of, 15, 18, 19,
  20, 23, 38, 41, 81, 83, 88, 124, 141,
  143, 170, 180
Copernicus, 7, 57, 68, 85, 92, 94, 95,
  120, 132, 162, 180, 189, 190
Coronensis, M., 87
Cracow, 194
Craig, 104, 181

Dancey, Charles, 42, 44, 57, 59, 60,
  62, 104
David, 17, 78
David, Psalms of, 16
Dekent, J. H., 87
Diogenes, 42
Doberau, 152
Dona, 174
Drake, 7
Dresden, 134, 165
Dryer, J. L. E., 24, 59, 79, 87, 95,
  130, 190, 193

East Friesland, 176
Ebenthood, C. N. de, 87
Edinburgh Castle, 118
Edinburgh Observatory, 113
Elbe, 165, 171, 173, 174
Elizabeth, Queen, 106, 119
Elizabeth of Denmark, 118, 121
Elsinore, 13, 58, 61, 63, 120
Engelholm, 62
Erasmus, 56
d'Eresby, Lord Willoughby, 106
Erik XIV, of Sweden, 28, 47
Eriksholm, 88
Eskild, Archbishop, 39
Eton, 131

Fabricus, 130, 173, 176
Femern, 99
Ferdinand, Archduke, 175
Fischer, P., 102

Flemløs, P. J., 87, 88, 92, 129
Foss, Anders, 93
Francis I, 26, 44
Frandsen, Hans, 40, 93, 100
Frangipani, 44
Frankfort, 55, 109, 112
Franklin Institute, 134
Frauenberg, 132
Frederick II, 3, 4, 15, 17, 18, 21, 28,
  36, 43, 44, 47, 53, 57, 59, 60, 63,
  66, 70, 75, 76, 77, 78, 79, 80, 81,
  82, 83, 86, 99, 102, 105, 107, 108,
  123, 124, 132, 145, 158, 160, 181
Frederick the Wise, 33
Fredriksborg, 58, 59, 64, 76
Friis, Christian, 137
Friis, F. R., 92
Friis, Johan, 4, 21, 43, 139
Frobenius, M. J., 88
Fuggers, 36

Galileo, 7, 25, 93, 95, 189
Gaschitz, 129
Gassendi, 19, 91
Gemperlin, Tobias, 56, 65, 112, 113
Geyn, 112, 133
Gjøe, Falk, 100
Glostrup, Niels, 188
Göggingen, 37
Goliath, 78
Gotha, 134
Gothenburg, 134
Grabow, 101
Graz, 175, 177
Guise, 5, 112
Gustavus Adolphus, 11, 78, 138
Gyldenkrone, Governor, 87
Gyldenstierne, Axel, 84, 123, 131, 163

Haderslebiensis, P. R., 87
Hagecius, Thaddæus, 57, 84, 165, 169
Hainzel, J. B., 36, 55, 104, 129
Hainzel, Paul, 36, 37, 162
Hamar, 93
Hamburg, 3, 160, 173
Hampton Court, 67
Hans, 80, 108
Hanseatic League, 3, 4, 35, 60
Hansen, Ejler, 23
Hegelius, J., 87
Heidelberg, 19, 21
Helsingborg, 13, 84, 137
Helvaderus, N., 101
Hemmingsen, Niels, 16, 17, 87
Henry II, 26, 44
Herlein, 188

Herrevad, Abbey of, 39, 40, 47, 99, 110
Herwarto of Hohenheim, 105
Hessen, 141
Hipparchus, 68
Hoffman, Baron, 176, 177, 178
Holberg, Ludwig, 49
Holk, Henrik, 83, 124
Holland, 3
Holstein, 3, 176
Holstein, Duke of, 99
Homalius, Johannes, 23, 176
Horsens, 99
Hradschin, 179
Huitfeld, Arild, 43
Hveen, 39, 58, 59, 60, 61, 62, 64, 69,
   81, 84, 86, 91, 95, 99, 113, 117,
   118, 119, 120, 121, 123, 124, 126,
   127, 129, 130, 134, 137, 142, 144,
   152, 154, 155, 156, 159, 160, 161,
   164, 173, 174, 188, 189, 192

Ibstrup, 58
Inquisition, 7
Isaac, 17
Islandus, O. W., 87

Jacobsen, Marius, 88
James VI (I), 118, 119, 120, 121,
   128
Janson, Wilhelm, 35
Jeppe, 13, 90, 91, 112
Jessen, Johannes, 165, 177, 187
Joachim, 100
Jørgensen, Hans, 16
Jørgensen, Morten, 16, 17, 18
Jutland, 21, 99, 108

Kaas, Niels, 4, 71, 93, 100, 105, 108,
   109, 123
Kalundborg, 13
Kalmar, Union of, 4
Keith, Lord, 118
Kepler, 7, 25, 40, 91, 95, 111, 174,
   175, 176, 177, 178, 181, 185, 189,
   190, 191
Knieper, Hans, 66
Knudstrup, 12, 13, 14, 39, 47, 57, 58,
   59, 83, 89, 92, 102, 110, 145, 152
Køge, 188
Krabbe, Tage, 42
Krag, Dr., 21, 142
Kronborg, 63, 64, 66, 76, 118, 131
Kullagaarden, 82, 139

Labkowitz, 179
Landskrona, 61, 84, 104, 137

Lange, Erik, 89, 93, 140, 171
Larivière, 26
Laubenwolf, 67
Laurentius, 179
Leipzig, 19, 21, 22, 23, 27, 28, 33
Leitmeritz, 174
Lemwicensis, A. J., 87
Leonardo, 131
Leyden, 19, 92, 160, 162, 192
Liddel, Duncan, 121
Longomontanus, K. S., 87, 91, 105,
   129, 149, 173, 176, 180
Louis XIV, 26
Louvre, 67
Lübeck, 35, 174
Lübeck, Archbishop of, 161, 162
Lund, University of, 69, 143, 145, 189
Luther, Martin, 5, 13, 33, 48
Lyndsay, David, 119

Madsen, Bishop, 131
Magdeburg, 173, 174
Magini, 105
Major, Johannes, 55, 84, 92, 104
Malmö, 13
Malmogiensis, J. N., 87
Månsdotter, Karin, 47
Mary, Queen of Scots, 101
Mathias, Archduke and King, 77, 162,
   194
Maximilian II, 169
Mecklenburg, Duke of, 110, 121, 152
Mecklenburg-Schwerin, 35, 101
Medici, 7, 25, 26
Medici, Catherine de, 26
Melanchthon, 16, 26, 33, 165
Michelangelo, 7, 131
Mikkelsen, Skipper, 38
Minichova, 134
Minkowitz, Ernfried, 186
Montmorency, Anne de, 44
Montpellier, 19
Morin, 26
Moritz, of Hesse-Cassel, 133, 162
Moritz, of Orange, 160
Morsing, E. O., 92
Mortensen, Harald, 37
Moryson, Fynes, 49
Moses, 95
Mühlstein, Kaspar von, 172
Mule, Klaus, 130, 173
Müller, J., 176
Munk, Peder, 108, 118, 131
Mylius, Dr., 55

Nelleman, J., 49

Neustadt, 101
Newton, 189, 191
Nilsson, 93
Nordfjord, 82, 109, 139, 156, 164
Nordlind, Wilhelm, 57, 104
Nôtredame, Michel, 26
Noyes, Alfred, 22
Nuremberg, 36, 67, 161

Odense, 5, 99, 113
Ohr, Philip von, 160
Olden-Barneveld, 160
Oldenburg, House of, 4
Oldenburg, Line of, 124
Orange, Prince of, 162
Orkney Islands, 119
Oslo, 93
Oxe, Inger, 13, 35, 134
Oxe, Peder, 4, 36, 43, 44, 151
Oxford, 19

Padua, 19, 26
Palladio, 56
Paris, 19
Parsbjerg, Manderup, 34, 35, 77
Paschen, Hans van, 62, 63
Patavinus, 161
Pedersen, Rasmus, 124
Pennsylvania, 134
Peucer, Kaspar, 33, 105
Pilsen, 165
Plantin, Christopher, 55
Pontanus, J. I., 87
Prague, 21, 38, 67, 111, 141, 162, 165, 169, 170, 171, 172, 177, 178, 179, 180, 187, 193, 194
Prague, University of, 27, 55, 88, 134, 165, 169
Pratensis, Johannes, 40, 42, 44, 54, 57, 59, 91, 100
Pré, Philippe de, 44
Ptolemy, 20, 22, 27, 28, 68, 92, 93, 95, 180
Pürglitz, 194

Raabeløb, 29
Raleigh, Sir Walter, 112
Ramus, Peter, 38
Rantzau, Breide, 118
Rantzau, Gert, 131
Rantzau, Henrik, 4, 43, 93, 100, 105, 151, 158, 159, 160, 164, 165
Rantzau, Johan, 158
Regensburg, 56, 57
Regiomontanus, 131
Reinhold, Erasmus, 24

Reventlov, Ditlev, 79
Reymarus, Nicholas, 131, 139
Rhodius, A., 88
Ribe, 21, 40, 93
Ripensis, C. J., 87
Rogers, Daniel, 106
Rome, 15, 42, 128, 129
Rosenberg, Peter Vok von, 185
Rosenborg, 64
Rosenkrantz, Holger, 104, 131, 161, 164, 180
Rosenkrantz, Jørgen, 4, 71, 108, 109, 123
Rosenspar, 163
Roskilde, 17, 36, 83, 86, 124, 125, 134, 139, 156
Rostock, 19, 34, 35, 76, 100, 151, 152, 154, 155, 158, 162
Rothmann, 105, 107, 121, 133, 176
Rubens, 7
Rud, 188
Rude, 163
Rudolph, Emperor, 38, 56, 84, 107, 113, 122, 160, 161, 165, 169, 170, 173, 174, 176, 178, 180, 181, 186, 194
Ruggieri, 26
Rumphæus, 170

Salamanca, 19
Salzburg, Archbishop of, 162
Sansovino, 179
Sascerides, D. J., 87, 141
Sascerides, Gellius, 87, 141, 142, 143, 193
Savoy, House of, 26
Saxony, Elector of, 33
Scaliger, J. J., 92, 105, 160, 162
Scania, 3, 13, 19, 29, 54, 57, 113, 143, 189
Schmalkaldian League, 173
Schönfeld, Victorinus, 88
Scultetus Batholomaeus, 23, 27, 105
Seccerwitz, 105
Sehested, Steen Maltesen, 71
Severinus, N., 87
Severinus, Peder, 122, 126
Shakespeare, 7
Shetland Islands, 119
Silesia, 38
Sjælland, 13, 18, 58, 143, 188, 189
Skram, Peder, 4, 78
Slesvig, 3
Solomon, 17
Sønderborg, 108

Sophia, Queen, 13, 21, 75, 79, 106, 119, 128, 158
Sorø, 81, 131
Sparre, Gustaf, 194
Spenser, 7
St. Bartholomew, 7, 38, 41, 44
St. Ib, Church of, 69
Stadius, Johann, 20, 23
Stella, Paolo della, 179
Stenwinckel, Hans van, 63, 68
Stjerneborg, 68, 69, 70, 85, 120, 132, 133, 138, 161
Stralsund, 38
Strassburg, 140
Sturtz, 105
Styria, 175
Suleiman, Sultan, 35

Tenfelt, von, 77
Tengnagel, F. G., 88, 105, 149, 160, 173, 176, 177, 180, 186, 193
Thau, Valentin, 23
Thott, Otte, 89
Thott, Tage, 89
Timocharis, 68
Titian, 7
Tostrup, 15, 29
Traubson, 170
Trolle, Herluf, 4, 28, 43, 163
Tübinger, 19
Tuna, 69

Ugerup, Arild, 84, 123
Ulfeld, Jacob, 43
Ulfstand, 163, 188
Ulrich of Mecklenburg, 79
Ulrik, 38, 44, 80, 131

United Provinces, 7
Uraniborg, 60, 62, 65, 68, 69, 70, 71, 84, 85, 86, 88, 90, 93, 100, 101, 105, 109, 110, 111, 112, 117, 120, 121, 123, 127, 128, 130, 131, 132, 133, 138, 139, 140, 141, 144, 145, 161, 174
Utichius, Paulus, 88, 93, 121

Valkendorf, Christofer, 4, 60, 75, 108, 117, 138, 139, 164
Valois, 7, 126
Vandaas, 29
Vedel, Anders Sorensen, 21, 22, 23, 28, 39, 44, 92, 99, 104, 107, 108, 109, 170
Vejle, 21, 131
Venice, 56, 122
Veronese, 7
Vienna, 92, 93, 103, 128, 134
Vindstrup, Bishop, 145

Wandsbeck, 158, 159, 162, 163, 164, 165
Wedgewood, C. V., 138
Weida, Christopher, 99, 129
Westphalia, 180
Wiburgensis, Andreas, 87
William of Courland, 121
William IV of Hesse-Cassel, 27, 54, 57, 104, 105, 107, 108, 133, 162
Wittenberg, 19, 21, 26, 28, 33, 34, 36, 100, 141, 158, 165, 173, 187
Wittich, Paul, 88, 93, 121
Wolf, Hieronymus, 104

Xenophon, 92